MONEY AND THE HARVEST

PASTOR DR. CLAUDINE BENJAMIN

MONEY AND THE HARVEST. Copyright @ 2025. Pastor Dr. Claudine Benjamin. All rights reserved.

For more information or to book an event, contact: inspiredtowinsouls@gmail.com

No part of this publication may be reproduced, stored in a retrieval system or transmitted in any form or by any means, electronic, mechanical, photocopying, recording or otherwise without the prior written permission of the author.

Published by:

Editor: Cleveland O. McLeish (Author C. Orville McLeish)

ISBN: 978-1-965635-47-6 (paperback)

Unless otherwise stated, all Scripture quotations are taken from the King James Version (KJV).

Scripture quotations marked "KJV" are taken from the Holy Bible, King James Version (Public Domain).

Scripture quotations marked (NIV) are taken from the Holy Bible, New International Version®, NIV®. Copyright © 1973, 1978, 1984 by Biblica, Inc.™ Used by permission of Zondervan. All rights reserved worldwide.

Scripture quotations marked (NLT) are taken from the Holy Bible, New Living Translation, copyright © 1996, 2004, 2007 by Tyndale House Foundation. Used by permission of Tyndale House Publishers, Inc., Carol Stream, Illinois 60188. All rights reserved.

Scripture quotations marked "NKJV" are taken from the New King James Version. Copyright © 1982 by Thomas Nelson, Inc. Used by permission. All rights reserved. Bible text from the New King James Version® is not to be reproduced in copies or otherwise by any means except as permitted in writing by Thomas Nelson, Inc., Attn: Bible Rights and Permissions, P.O. Box 141000, Nashville, TN 37214-1000.

Scripture quotations marked "ESV" are from the ESV Bible® (The Holy Bible, English Standard Version®), copyright © 2001 by Crossway Bibles, a publishing ministry of Good News Publishers. Used by permission. All rights reserved.

Scripture quotations taken from the Amplified® Bible (AMP). Copyright © 2015 by The Lockman Foundation. Used by permission. www.Lockman.org.

About the Author

Pastor Claudine Benjamin is a passionate kingdom leader, prophetic voice, and devoted servant of God, called to challenge, equip, and mobilize the church in this urgent hour. With a clear mandate to preach the gospel, ignite revival, and awaken the body of Christ to the reality of the harvest, she is a respected voice in both spiritual and practical spheres of ministry.

As the founder of a dynamic ministry rooted in evangelism, intercession, and discipleship, Pastor Claudine has dedicated her life to the advancement of God's kingdom. Her messages are uncompromising, Spirit-led, and anchored in biblical truth. Through conferences, books, training sessions, and personal mentorship, she has equipped believers around the world to step into their calling with faith, authority, and financial purpose.

In Money and the Harvest, Pastor Claudine prophetically challenges the church to break free from consumer-based Christianity and embrace kingdom stewardship. She believes that God's people must be more than spiritual—they must be strategic. Finances are not just about budgets; they are about building altars, sending laborers, and reaching souls. Her passion for soul-winning is deeply woven throughout her teachings, with an emphasis on the responsibility of believers to fund what heaven values most.

Her ministry is characterized by a deep love for the Word, fervent prayer, and a profound concern for the lost. She is committed to raising up bold, generous, and Spirit-filled harvesters who view wealth as a tool of revival, not merely a symbol of success.

Beyond the platform and the pulpit, Pastor Claudine is a devoted and loving mother, as well as a faithful family leader. Her family is the foundation of her ministry, and together, they model what it means to serve God with humility, strength, and unity. Children and grandchildren are her greatest joy and legacy. As a family, they understand the cost of the calling, and they walk together in faith, purpose, and obedience.

Whether writing, teaching, or leading, Pastor Claudine's heart is the same: to see lives transformed, churches awakened, and the gospel funded until every soul has heard.

Dedication

This book is dedicated to every kingdom laborer who understands the divine connection between sowing and reaping—between financial stewardship and spiritual harvest.

To those who have sacrificed in secret, given without applause, and sown with tears—you are heaven's investors, and your reward is both eternal and undeniable.

To the faithful tithers, generous givers, and obedient sowers—your partnership with the purposes of God is not forgotten. This work is a tribute to your unseen labor, your unwavering faith, and your love for the advancement of God's kingdom.

And to future kingdom financiers—those being raised up to fund revivals, missions, churches, and global outreach—may this book stir a fire in you to rise in purpose and provision.

Acknowledgment

With a heart full of gratitude, I give honor to God, the Source of all wisdom, the Owner of all wealth, and the Lord of the harvest. This book would not exist without the Spirit of God stirring the urgency of this message within me. To Him belongs all glory, now and forever.

I also extend my deepest gratitude to every pastor, teacher, and kingdom leader who has stood on the front lines, teaching biblical financial principles with integrity and boldness. Your courage to speak the truth about money, stewardship, and the church's responsibility in this generation has ignited a revival in both resources and souls.

To my mentors and spiritual coverings—thank you for modeling faithful stewardship and unwavering trust in God's provision. Your prayers, counsel, and support have helped shape the message within these pages.

To my family—your patience, encouragement, and belief in the call of God on my life have made this journey possible. You are my blessing and my strength.

And to every reader, minister, marketplace believer, and kingdom builder reading this: thank you for investing your time into this divine revelation. May this book challenge, equip, and activate you to walk in divine purpose—not just with your heart, but with your hands and resources.

The harvest is plentiful. The time is now. Let us arise as faithful stewards and kingdom financiers—because money and the harvest go hand in hand.

Vision Statement: Why We Give?

We give because God gave first.

We sow because the harvest is ready.

We fund the mission because the gospel is not meant to stay silent, stalled, or limited by lack.

Our vision is to see every believer become a kingdom financier, every church become a sending station, and every soul within reach of the transforming power of Jesus Christ.

We do not give out of pressure, guilt, or religious ritual.

We give with purpose, on purpose—for the cause of Christ and the souls He died to save.

Table of Contents

About the Author iii
Dedication v
Acknowledgment vii
Vision Statement: Why We Give? ix
Introduction: Financing the Mission of God 13

Part 1

The Purpose of Money in the Kingdom

Chapter 1: Kingdom Currency – What Is Money For? 17

Chapter 2: The Economy of Heaven vs. the Economy of Earth .. 25

Chapter 3: God Funds His Own Mission 29

Part 2

The Relationship Between Money and the Harvest

Chapter 4: The Gospel Isn't Free—It Was Paid For 37

Chapter 5: Funding the Great Commission 41

Chapter 6: Generosity That Fuels Revival 45

Part 3

Breaking Financial Bondage for the Sake of the Harvest

Chapter 7: The Spirit of Mammon vs. the Spirit of God 69

Chapter 8: Poverty, Prosperity, and Purpose 77

Chapter 9: Debt, Distraction, and Delay in the Harvest 83

Part 4

Becoming a Harvest Financier

Chapter 10: You Are God's Banker 95

Chapter 11: Sowing Seeds That Reap Souls 105

Chapter 12: Strategic Giving for Strategic Harvests 113

Part 5

A Call to Harvest Partnership

Chapter 13: The Anointing of the Harvest Sponsor 125

Chapter 14: The Church That Funds the Harvest 135

Chapter 15: The Eternal Return on Investment 145

Conclusion: Giving That Outlives You 155

Harvest Declarations and Promises 163

Harvest Promises from God's Word 165

Call to Action: Your Hands Hold the Answer 167

Scripture and Reference Index 169

Introduction

Financing the Mission of God

The great commission is the greatest assignment ever given to the church—and it requires more than just prayer, preaching, and passion. It requires provision. While salvation is free, the spread of the gospel has always come with a cost. From the early church in Acts to the present-day missions field, the advancement of God's kingdom has always needed willing hearts—and resourced hands.

God's mission is to reach the world with the message of Christ, to disciple nations, and to establish His church in every generation. But that mission cannot move forward without the faithful and sacrificial giving of those who understand their financial role in God's eternal agenda. Giving is not a side matter in the kingdom—it is a central component of revival, outreach, and transformation.

The pages that follow are not just about money—they are about obedience. They are about recognizing that everything we have has been entrusted to us by God, not for comfort or consumption alone, but for the sake of the kingdom commission. We are stewards of divine resources, called to fund the harvest, fuel evangelism, and ensure that the gospel does not remain local—but goes global.

Pastor Dr. Claudine Benjamin

This is a call to pastors, leaders, churches, and every believer who dares to ask: What more can I do to support God's work? It is a prophetic invitation to align your wallet with your worship, your bank account with your burden for souls, and your financial decisions with your faith.

Financing the mission of God is not just a matter of generosity—it is a matter of urgency. The time is now. The harvest is ready. And God is calling us to release what is in our hands so He can accomplish what is in His heart.

Part 1

The Purpose of Money

in the Kingdom

Chapter 1

Kingdom Currency – What Is Money For?

In the natural world, money is used to exchange goods and services. But in the kingdom of God, money becomes more than a transaction tool—it becomes a resource for revelation, restoration, and the reaching of souls. When placed in the hands of the righteous, money becomes a weapon against darkness, a builder of the church, and a catalyst for the harvest.

Money Is a Tool, Not a Master

Too many believers either idolize money or demonize it. But scripture reminds us that money is neither inherently good nor evil—it simply reflects the heart of the one who holds it.

> **"For the love of money is the root of all evil: which while some coveted after, they have erred from the faith, and pierced themselves through with many sorrows."** —1 Timothy 6:10 (KJV)

Money becomes dangerous when it governs your decisions instead of God. Yet, when surrendered to the Lord, it becomes a powerful tool for advancing His purposes.

Pastor Dr. Claudine Benjamin

God's Original Design for Provision

From the beginning, God intended that His people would walk in provision, not in lack. He gave Adam and Eve everything they needed to thrive. Provision was always tied to purpose.

> **"But thou shalt remember the Lord thy God: for it is he that giveth thee power to get wealth…"** —Deuteronomy 8:18a (KJV)

The ability to gain wealth is not just for comfort but for covenant fulfillment. It's about resourcing kingdom vision.

In the kingdom, money is not the goal—it is a tool to fulfill the goal. It helps build churches, send missionaries, fund outreaches, feed the hungry, clothe the poor, and empower the spread of the gospel.

> **"No man can serve two masters… Ye cannot serve God and mammon."** —Matthew 6:24 (KJV)

Money is a wonderful servant but a terrible master. The purpose of money is to advance God's purposes, not to enslave God's people.

Stewardship vs. Ownership

One of the biggest mistakes we make is assuming ownership of what we merely manage. In the kingdom, we are not owners—we are stewards. A steward manages the resources of another.

> **"Moreover it is required in stewards, that a man be found faithful."** —1 Corinthians 4:2 (KJV)

God wants to bless faithful stewards who understand that every dollar is a divine deposit, entrusted to serve a heavenly mission.

Money as a Kingdom Assignment

Money is never neutral in the kingdom. When God places wealth in your hands, it comes with an assignment—to fund the message of the gospel, to support the poor, to feed the hungry, and to rescue the lost.

> **"Charge them that are rich in this world, that they be not highminded, nor trust in uncertain riches, but in the living God, who giveth us richly all things to enjoy; That they do good, that they be rich in good works, ready to distribute, willing to communicate;" —1 Timothy 6:17–18 (KJV)**

The more you understand this, the more you will see yourself not just as a believer—but as a kingdom financier.

Biblical Examples of Money Used for Mission

- Joseph of Arimathea used his wealth to bury Jesus in a new tomb (see Matthew 27:57–60).
- Lydia, a seller of purple cloth, supported the ministry of Paul (see Acts 16:14–15).
- The women who followed Jesus, such as Joanna and Susanna, financially supported His ministry (see Luke 8:1–3).

These were not just donors—they were partners in the harvest.

Money, when rightly understood and properly used, becomes a divine instrument in the hands of the believer. In the kingdom of

God, money is not merely for comfort or personal gain—it is a tool of stewardship, a weapon of warfare, and a seed for the harvest. God never intended for money to rule us, but rather that we would rule over it and use it to accomplish His will on the earth.

Money Enables Mission

The mission of the church cannot move forward without resources. While salvation is free, the work of the gospel has real costs—travel, materials, technology, training, relief efforts, and more.

> **"How shall they preach, except they be sent?" —Romans 10:15 (KJV)**

God uses the finances of His people to send the gospel to places they may never go, making every giver a vital part of the mission.

God Blesses for Purpose

God does not bless us with wealth to indulge our desires—He blesses us to fulfill His covenant and purpose.

When you understand that your financial increase is connected to God's mission, you position yourself to be a vessel of blessing, not just a recipient of it.

Stewardship is a Kingdom Mandate

Every dollar that passes through our hands is a test of our stewardship. Will we consume it, waste it, or invest it into the eternal purposes of God?

Stewardship is not just about what we give—it's about how we manage everything God gives us. When we handle money with kingdom wisdom, we unlock heaven's flow through our lives.

Money Funds the Harvest

Jesus said the harvest is plentiful, but the laborers are few (see Matthew 9:37). Part of the reason is that the laborers often lack funding. Money allows ministries to be mobilized, workers to be trained, and doors to be opened.

> **"The liberal soul shall be made fat: and he that watereth shall be watered also himself." —Proverbs 11:25 (KJV)**

When you use your money to fund the harvest, you become part of a spiritual transaction that impacts both earth and eternity.

Money Tests the Heart

Jesus spoke more about money than He did about heaven and hell—not because He was after our wallets, but because money reveals the heart.

> **"For where your treasure is, there will your heart be also." —Matthew 6:21 (KJV)**

How we use money shows what we truly value. God watches not just the amount we give but the motive behind it.

Pastor Dr. Claudine Benjamin

Money is a Seed with Multiplying Power

When given in faith and obedience, money becomes a seed that multiplies into souls, salvations, and spiritual impact.

> **"He which soweth bountifully shall reap also bountifully."**
> **—2 Corinthians 9:6 (KJV)**

> **"Now he that ministereth seed to the sower... multiply your seed sown, and increase the fruits of your righteousness."**
> **—2 Corinthians 9:10 (KJV)**

When your finances align with God's heart, supernatural multiplication takes place. You sow on earth and reap in eternity.

Reflection Questions

1. Do you see money as a tool for kingdom purposes or personal gain?

2. Are you managing your resources in a way that pleases God?

3. How much of your income is being invested in the mission of the gospel?

4. Do you view money as a spiritual tool?

5. Are you faithful with what God has given you?

6. How is your money being used to advance the harvest?

Prayer

Lord, I thank You for every resource You've entrusted to me. Help me to see money the way You see it—not as a source of identity, but as a tool for kingdom impact. Make me a faithful steward, a cheerful giver, and a wise investor in the things that matter most. Use my finances to reach the lost and build Your church. In Jesus' name. Amen.

Chapter 2

The Economy of Heaven vs. the Economy of Earth

We are living in a time when earthly economies are shaking—stock markets fluctuate, currencies lose value, and inflation destabilizes nations. But the economy of heaven is unshakable. It operates on principles of faith, obedience, and supernatural provision, not on supply chains or interest rates.

God is calling His people to shift their trust from the systems of man to the kingdom of God.

The Earthly System: Fear, Greed, and Control

The world's financial system is rooted in fear: fear of lack, fear of poverty, and fear of not having enough. It promotes greed, hoarding, and selfishness.

> **"The Lord knoweth the thoughts of man, that they are vanity." —Psalm 94:11 (KJV)**

Earthly wealth is uncertain and easily lost. Jesus warned us about storing treasure where moth and rust corrupt.

> "Lay not up for yourselves treasures upon earth, where moth and rust doth corrupt, and where thieves break through and steal." —Matthew 6:19 (KJV)

God does not want His people to be dependent on fragile systems. He offers a higher economy—an economy of trust.

Heaven's Economy: Faith, Obedience, and Overflow

Heaven's economy is not based on how much you have but on how much you trust.

> "But my God shall supply all your need according to his riches in glory by Christ Jesus." —Philippians 4:19 (KJV)

The kingdom economy is governed by giving, not hoarding. In the natural, giving reduces your supply. In the supernatural, giving multiplies your harvest.

> "Give, and it shall be given unto you; good measure, pressed down, and shaken together, and running over…" —Luke 6:38 (KJV)

Faith activates the flow of provision. When you operate in faith, God becomes your source—not your job, paycheck, or savings account.

God's Provision in Famine and Crisis

Throughout scripture, God proved that His economy overrides earthly circumstances:

Money and the Harvest

- Elijah was fed by ravens and later by a widow in Zarephath during a drought (see 1 Kings 17:6).
- Isaac sowed in famine and reaped a hundredfold in the same year (see Genesis 26:12).
- The Israelites ate manna from heaven for 40 years in the wilderness (see Exodus 16).

> "I have been young, and now am old; yet have I not seen the righteous forsaken, nor his seed begging bread." — **Psalm 37:25 (KJV)**

God's economy functions outside of natural limitations.

Faith Is the Currency of the Kingdom

In the world, you need cash or credit. In the kingdom, faith is your currency. Faith unlocks resources. Faith provokes miracles. Faith makes what seems impossible suddenly available.

> "Now faith is the substance of things hoped for, the evidence of things not seen." —**Hebrews 11:1 (KJV)**

When you operate in kingdom faith, you're not limited by what you see. You're resourced by what God says.

Aligning with Heaven's Financial Flow

To access God's economy, we must align our priorities:

- Seek first the kingdom

> "But seek ye first the kingdom of God, and his righteousness; and all these things shall be added unto

you." —Matthew 6:33 (KJV)

- Honor God with your resources

"Honour the Lord with thy substance, and with the firstfruits of all thine increase." —Proverbs 3:9 (KJV)

- Trust and obey without fear

"Trust in the Lord with all thine heart; and lean not unto thine own understanding." —Proverbs 3:5 (KJV)

Reflection Questions

1. Are you trusting in the world's system or God's promises?

2. Do you see your giving as an act of faith?

3. Are you aligning with kingdom principles or earthly fears?

Prayer

Father, help me to trust Your economy even when the world's system is unstable. Teach me to walk by faith, to give with obedience, and to believe for supernatural provision. May my finances reflect Your kingdom—not my fear. In Jesus' name. Amen.

Chapter 3

God Funds His Own Mission

God never launches a mission without provision. From Genesis to Revelation, we see a divine pattern: when God gives vision, He sends provision. He does not depend on earthly systems or man's ability—He funds His mission by placing resources into the hands of obedient vessels. The harvest is God's priority, and He will not allow His work to go unfunded.

He Owns It All

The foundation of divine provision is the understanding that God owns everything. We are not the source—we are the stewards.

> "The earth is the Lord's, and the fulness thereof; the world, and they that dwell therein." —Psalm 24:1 (KJV)

> "For every beast of the forest is mine, and the cattle upon a thousand hills." —Psalm 50:10 (KJV)

Because God owns all things, He can release provision at any moment, through any means, to fund His purposes.

Pastor Dr. Claudine Benjamin

Provision Always Follows Purpose

God never provides randomly—He provides in alignment with His purpose. When we align ourselves with God's heart for the lost, resources begin to flow.

> **"According as his divine power hath given unto us all things that pertain unto life and godliness…"** —2 Peter 1:3 (KJV)

The ministries that walk in the greatest provision are often those who are closest to the heart of God's mission: the harvest.

God Funds His Work Through People

Although God owns all resources, He chooses to use people as channels to fund the mission. Throughout scripture, He raised up faithful financiers for His cause:

- The Tabernacle of Moses was built through freewill offerings from the people (see Exodus 35:4–5).
- The Temple of Solomon was funded by David's generous giving and the wealth of Israel (see 1 Chronicles 29:2–9).
- Jesus' earthly ministry was supported by women and followers who gave consistently (see Luke 8:1–3).
- Paul's missionary journeys were made possible through the faithful support of people like the Philippians (see Philippians 4:15–18).

> **"Every man according as he purposeth in his heart, so let him give…for God loveth a cheerful giver."** —2 Corinthians 9:7 (KJV)

God blesses His people not just for personal gain but to be a blessing for the advancement of His kingdom.

Divine Supply for Divine Assignments

When God sends you, He sustains you. The Bible is filled with moments when God miraculously provided for His people because they were on assignment:

- Elijah received bread and meat from ravens by the brook (see 1 Kings 17:4–6).
- The widow of Zarephath was sustained through divine multiplication during a famine because she gave first (see 1 Kings 17:13–16).
- Jesus fed the 5,000 with five loaves and two fish to sustain the crowd that had gathered to hear the gospel (see Matthew 14:16–21).

"But my God shall supply all your need according to his riches in glory by Christ Jesus." —Philippians 4:19 (KJV)

When you walk in obedience, you become the recipient of heaven's provision.

Lack Never Cancels the Mission

Some believe that if there are not enough resources, the mission must be paused. But the Bible shows us that lack is not a valid excuse when God has given a command.

"And he said unto them, Go ye into all the world, and preach the gospel to every creature." —Mark 16:15 (KJV)

Jesus never told His disciples to wait for perfect funding. He told them to go—and in going, they experienced miracles of provision.

> **"And he said unto them, When I sent you without purse, and scrip, and shoes, lacked ye any thing? And they said, Nothing." —Luke 22:35 (KJV)**

The Church Must Stop Saying "We Don't Have Enough"

Many churches and believers have become paralyzed by fear of insufficiency. But when the focus shifts to God's ability rather than man's limitations, faith releases the necessary supply.

> **"Is any thing too hard for the Lord?" —Genesis 18:14 (KJV)**

God is looking for churches and individuals who will believe Him for supernatural provision for the sake of the harvest.

Reflection Questions

1. Are you trusting God to provide the funding for what He has called you to do?

2. Have you made excuses based on finances instead of trusting His faithfulness?

3. Are you willing to be a vessel God can use to finance His mission?

Prayer

Father, I thank You that You are the God who funds Your own mission. Teach me to walk in faith, not fear. Use me as a channel of provision for Your kingdom. Let my hands be open to give, and my heart be aligned with Your purpose for the harvest. In Jesus' name. Amen.

Part 2

The Relationship Between

Money and the Harvest

Chapter 4

The Gospel Isn't Free—It Was Paid For

Many say, "Salvation is free," and while that is true for the recipient, it is not free to provide. The gospel came at the highest cost—the life of Jesus Christ—and its advancement continues to require sacrifice, obedience, and financial support. The church must awaken to the reality that the spread of the gospel demands investment—spiritual and financial.

Salvation Was Paid for with Blood

The gospel is not cheap. It cost the Father His Son and the Son His life.

> **"For ye are bought with a price: therefore glorify God in your body, and in your spirit, which are God's." —1 Corinthians 6:20 (KJV)**

> **"But God commendeth his love toward us, in that, while we were yet sinners, Christ died for us." —Romans 5:8 (KJV)**

Every soul saved is the result of a price already paid. The church must never cheapen the gospel by treating it as effortless. Grace is free to us, but it costs God everything.

Pastor Dr. Claudine Benjamin

Spreading the Gospel Costs Resources

While salvation is already purchased, spreading the message involves tangible costs. Bibles must be printed, churches planted, missionaries sent, outreach events held, and ministries maintained.

> **"How then shall they call on him in whom they have not believed?...And how shall they preach, except they be sent?" —Romans 10:14–15 (KJV)**

Sending requires resources. Preaching incurs expense. Even Jesus, who had all power, operated a traveling ministry that required support.

Jesus' Ministry Had Financial Support

The Savior of the world allowed people to give into His ministry, teaching us that giving is part of participating in the mission.

> **"And certain women, which had been healed of evil spirits and infirmities...and many others, which ministered unto him of their substance." —Luke 8:2–3 (KJV)**

Jesus never rebuked those who supported Him financially. Instead, He welcomed their giving as a form of worship and partnership.

Paul the Apostle Was Honest About Financial Needs

Paul, one of the greatest evangelists, made it clear that gospel ministry required resources. He honored those who gave, especially the Philippian church:

> "Not because I desire a gift: but I desire fruit that may abound to your account." —Philippians 4:17 (KJV)

He knew their giving produced eternal results. In return, he spoke a prophetic promise over their finances:

> "But my God shall supply all your need according to his riches in glory by Christ Jesus." —Philippians 4:19 (KJV)

When we support the gospel, we are investing in eternity.

If the Church Doesn't Pay the Price, the Message Stalls

The gospel will not reach its full potential through mere good intentions. It must be funded, fueled, and furthered by believers who understand their role in the harvest.

> "The labourer is worthy of his reward." —1 Timothy 5:18 (KJV)

Every outreach, mission trip, and evangelistic effort needs funding. Souls are waiting—not for another sermon—but for a church willing to send and support.

Paying the Price Means Partnership with God

God's strategy has always been to involve His people in His work. He could finance it miraculously without us—but He chooses to work through willing vessels.

> "Bring ye all the tithes into the storehouse... and prove me now herewith, saith the Lord of hosts..." —Malachi 3:10 (KJV)

Pastor Dr. Claudine Benjamin

When you give to the gospel, you partner with heaven. You become part of the story of every soul reached, every life changed, every heart transformed.

Reflection Questions

1. Do you understand the cost of spreading the gospel?

2. Are you willing to be a financial partner in God's mission?

3. Have you viewed giving as worship and warfare?

Prayer

Lord, thank You for paying the ultimate price for my salvation. Let me never take that lightly. Use me as a vessel to support the gospel in every way You see fit. Teach me to give cheerfully, sacrificially, and with eternity in mind. Let my finances reflect my faith. In Jesus' name. Amen.

Chapter 5

Funding the Great Commission

The great commission is the church's mandate to reach the world with the gospel of Jesus Christ. Yet too often, churches are underfunded, missionaries are unsupported, and evangelism is sidelined—not because the harvest isn't ready, but because the church hasn't prioritized resourcing the mission. This chapter highlights the pressing need to financially support the great commission.

The Mission Is Global, but It Requires Local Investment

Jesus commanded the church to go to the ends of the earth, but that global command begins with local obedience—especially in our use of resources.

> "Go ye therefore, and teach all nations... teaching them to observe all things whatsoever I have commanded you." —Matthew 28:19–20 (KJV)

> "But ye shall receive power... and ye shall be witnesses unto me... unto the uttermost part of the earth." —Acts 1:8 (KJV)

Pastor Dr. Claudine Benjamin

We cannot fulfill a global mandate with a local mindset. Financial investment must reflect the magnitude of the mission.

The Commission Cannot Be Fulfilled Without Contribution

We often separate spiritual and financial responsibility—but in the kingdom, they are connected. Where your treasure is, your heart follows (see Matthew 6:21). If your heart is for souls, your finances should follow.

> **"Even so hath the Lord ordained that they which preach the gospel should live of the gospel." —1 Corinthians 9:14 (KJV)**

Those who go must be supported by those who send. The great commission is not for a few—it's for the entire body of Christ.

A Mission-Funding Church is a Harvest-Reaping Church

Churches that invest in outreach, missions, and evangelism tend to experience a greater impact and return. God blesses churches that put His priorities first.

> **"He that hath pity upon the poor lendeth unto the Lord; and that which he hath given will he pay him again." —Proverbs 19:17 (KJV)**

> **"There is that scattereth, and yet increaseth; and there is that withholdeth more than is meet, but it tendeth to poverty." —Proverbs 11:24 (KJV)**

Money and the Harvest

When a church loosens its grip on its funds to fund the harvest, God opens heaven over that ministry.

Missions Are the Heartbeat of God—And Should Be Funded Accordingly

Too often, churches spend more on buildings, programs, and comfort than on evangelism and missions. But God's priority has never changed: souls are His heart.

> "For the Son of man is come to seek and to save that which was lost." —Luke 19:10 (KJV)

If that's why Jesus came, then funding that mission should be our highest budget line.

Every Dollar Invested in Souls Produces Eternal Dividends

Giving to the great commission is not a donation—it's an eternal investment. When you sow into soul-winning, you lay up treasures in heaven.

> "But lay up for yourselves treasures in heaven… For where your treasure is, there will your heart be also." —Matthew 6:20–21 (KJV)

Your giving funds the gospel, plants churches, trains leaders, and reaches those who might never hear otherwise.

Pastor Dr. Claudine Benjamin

The Church Must Shift from Consumerism to Commission

Modern church culture often prioritizes entertainment and experience over engagement in mission. But the early church was focused on sending, reaching, and expanding the gospel.

"And how shall they preach, except they be sent?" — Romans 10:15 (KJV)

Sending costs money. Preaching costs money. Printing Bibles, training ministers, reaching the unreached—it all takes resources. We must shift from consumer Christians to contributing Christians.

Reflection Questions

1. How much of your giving is directed toward the great commission?

2. Is your church actively investing in outreach and soul-winning?

3. Do you see funding the gospel as a mandate, not a suggestion?

Prayer

Lord, I hear Your call to the nations and the lost. Let my heart burn for what burns Yours. Use my resources, church, and life to fund the great commission. Let every dollar I give be a seed that brings a soul into Your kingdom. In Jesus' name. Amen.

Chapter 6

Generosity That Fuels Revival

Revival is not just a spiritual event—it is a divine movement that transforms hearts, families, communities, and nations. While revival begins with prayer, repentance, and a return to God, it is sustained and expanded through generosity. A generous church is a powerful church, and revival cannot flourish where resources are withheld. God is calling His people to a level of generosity that ignites and sustains the harvest.

Revival Costs Something

Every revival in history has come with a price—prayer, sacrifice, time, and, yes, money. Events must be organized, venues rented, people reached, and resources distributed.

Revival is not cheap. It is not comfortable. It will never come to a complacent, passive, or lukewarm church. Every historic move of God has come at a cost—a cost of time, prayer, obedience, sacrifice, and surrender. We cannot expect heaven to open while we remain closed to the demands of the Spirit.

Revival may be free in grace, but it is never cheap in commitment.

1. *It Costs Personal Comfort*

Pastor Dr. Claudine Benjamin

Revival will disrupt your schedule, preferences, and routine. It will call you to uncomfortable places—early morning prayer, long nights of intercession, fasting when others are feasting. True revivalists are not driven by comfort; they are driven by calling.

Scriptures:

- "Woe to them that are at ease in Zion…" —Amos 6:1 (KJV)

- "Take up your cross daily and follow Me." (see Luke 9:23).

- "Present your bodies as a living sacrifice, holy and acceptable to God—this is your true and proper worship." (see Romans 12:1).

2. It Costs Reputation

Revivalists are often misunderstood, criticized, and rejected—even by religious people. When you begin to burn for God, not everyone will understand the fire within you. Revival separates the wheat from the chaff and exposes religious deadness.

Scriptures:

- "Blessed are you when people insult you, persecute you and falsely say all kinds of evil against you because of Me." —Matthew 5:11 (NIV)

- "Am I now trying to win the approval of human beings, or of God?" —Galatians 1:10 (NIV)

- **"The world hated Me before it hated you." (see John 15:18).**

3. *It Costs Financial Sacrifice*

Revival is resourced by the faithful giving of God's people. In the book of Acts, believers sold possessions and laid the proceeds at the apostles' feet to meet needs and advance the gospel. Today, revival requires kingdom financiers—those who understand that where their treasure is, there their heart will be also.

Scriptures:

- **"They sold property and possessions to give to anyone who had need." —Acts 2:45 (NIV)**

- **"Honor the Lord with your wealth, with the firstfruits of all your crops." —Proverbs 3:9 (NIV)**

- **"For where your treasure is, there your heart will be also." —Matthew 6:21 (NIV)**

4. *It Costs Deep Repentance*

Revival is birthed in brokenness. God does not revive the proud, the distracted, or the self-sufficient. He revives the contrite, hungry, and humble. We must come low before Him in deep repentance for personal sin and corporate apathy.

Scriptures:

- **"If my people, who are called by my name, will humble themselves and pray and seek my face and turn from** their wicked ways…" —2 Chronicles 7:14 (NIV)

- "The Lord is near to the brokenhearted and saves the crushed in spirit." —Psalm 34:18 (ESV)

- "Rend your heart and not your garments." —Joel 2:13 (NIV)

5. *It Costs Total Obedience*

Revival doesn't come where there's partial obedience. It comes where people are yielded, obedient, and surrendered to whatever God requires—no matter the cost. Revival calls you to go where others won't, give what others withhold, and say yes when others say no.

Scriptures:

- "To obey is better than sacrifice…" —1 Samuel 15:22 (NIV)

- "Here am I, send me." —Isaiah 6:8 (NIV)

- "Whatever He says to you, do it." —John 2:5 (NKJV)

Are You Willing to Pay the Price?

Every great revival has come through costly surrender. If we want heaven to open, fire to fall, and souls to flood the altar, then we must count the cost—and be willing to pay it. Revival will cost you something, but what it brings is priceless: lives transformed, families restored, and a church awakened to her purpose.

> "Neither will I offer burnt offerings unto the Lord my God of that which doth cost me nothing." —2 Samuel 24:24 (KJV)

Revival is costly, and God honors those who give generously to fuel His movement.

The Early Church: A Model of Radical Generosity

The early church did not merely believe in generosity—they embodied it. Their love for God overflowed in tangible acts of giving, sharing, and serving. Their financial priorities were not rooted in accumulation but in advancement—the advancement of the gospel, the care for the poor, and the building of a unified, Spirit-filled community.

This wasn't casual giving. This was radical generosity—costly, selfless, Spirit-led generosity that shook the foundations of society and demonstrated the heart of God.

1. *They Gave Freely and Frequently*

Generosity wasn't a one-time campaign in the early church; it was a lifestyle. Believers brought their resources together to meet needs as they arose—not because they were forced, but because they were filled with love.

Scriptures:

- "All the believers were together and had everything in common. They sold property and possessions to give to anyone who had need." —Acts 2:44–45 (NIV)

- "There were no needy persons among them. For from time to time those who owned land or houses sold them, brought the money... and it was distributed to anyone who had need." —Acts 4:34–35 (NIV)

Their giving was not driven by guilt—it was driven by grace.

2. *They Prioritized People Over Possessions*

In a culture of materialism, the early church showed that people mattered more than property. They understood that possessions were temporary, but the souls of men were eternal. Radical generosity wasn't about how much they gave—it was about how much they loved.

Scriptures:

- "Command them to do good, to be rich in good deeds, and to be generous and willing to share." —1 Timothy 6:18 (NIV)

- "Do nothing out of selfish ambition or vain conceit. Rather, in humility value others above yourselves, not looking to your own interests but each of you to the interests of the others." —Philippians 2:3-4 (NIV)

This heart posture created a culture of unity, trust, and mutual care.

3. *They Gave as an Act of Worship*

For the early believers, giving was never detached from worship—it was an integral part of worship. Offering their resources to God

Money and the Harvest

and to one another was a holy act, an extension of their devotion to Christ. They didn't just lift their hands—they opened their hands.

Scriptures:

- **"They broke bread in their homes and ate together with glad and sincere hearts, praising God…"** —Acts 2:46–47 (NIV)

- **"Honor the Lord with your wealth, with the firstfruits of all your crops."** —Proverbs 3:9 (NIV)

- **"For where your treasure is, there your heart will be also."** —Matthew 6:21 (NIV)

Their generosity was an offering that rose like incense before the throne of God.

4. *They Understood Kingdom Economics*

The early church operated in kingdom economics, where giving didn't subtract—it multiplied. They believed what Jesus taught: that when you give, it will be given back, pressed down, shaken together, and running over. They sowed into the Spirit, not into self.

Scriptures:

- **"Give, and it will be given to you. A good measure… will be poured into your lap…"** —Luke 6:38 (NIV)

- **"Whoever sows sparingly will also reap sparingly, and whoever sows generously will also reap generously."** —

2 Corinthians 9:6 (NIV)

- "And my God will meet all your needs according to the riches of his glory in Christ Jesus." —Philippians 4:19 (NIV)

They did not fear lack because they lived under the covering of divine provision.

5. *They Reflected the Heart of God*

Radical generosity is a reflection of God's own character. The early church imitated the generosity of the Father, who gave His only Son, and of the Son, who gave His life. To give sacrificially is to love deeply.

Scriptures:

- "For God so loved the world that He gave His one and only Son..." —John 3:16 (NIV)

- "You know the grace of our Lord Jesus Christ, that though He was rich, yet for your sake He became poor..." —2 Corinthians 8:9 (NIV)

- "Follow God's example, therefore, as dearly loved children." —Ephesians 5:1 (NIV)

The early church gave because they were transformed. They didn't just give to the church—they gave as the church.

A Call to Return

In today's world, the church must return to the radical generosity of Acts. Our faith must be visible in our giving. Our love must show in our stewardship. Our commitment to Christ must be evident in how we handle our finances—not for personal gain, but for the expansion of the kingdom.

Will we be like the early church? Will we give beyond reason, beyond comfort, beyond convenience—for the sake of the gospel?

The book of Acts gives us a vivid picture of a church on fire—spiritually powerful and radically generous.

> **"And the multitude of them that believed were of one heart and of one soul: neither said any of them that ought of the things which he possessed was his own… Neither was there any among them that lacked…" —Acts 4:32–34 (KJV)**

Their generosity wasn't driven by obligation—it was a natural overflow of revival. They shared everything, and the result was supernatural unity, miracles, and mass salvations.

Generosity is Fuel for Evangelism

Evangelism is the heartbeat of heaven—but generosity is the fuel that helps carry it forward on earth. While salvation is free, the work of reaching the lost is not. Tracts cost money. Missions cost money. Outreach events, gospel crusades, food drives, shelters, church plants, and Bibles for the unreached all require resources.

Pastor Dr. Claudine Benjamin

The early church knew this. Jesus' ministry reflected this. And today's church must return to this truth: generosity empowers evangelism.

1. *You Can't Send What You Don't Support*

Paul the Apostle could not have fulfilled his missionary journeys without the financial support of the early churches. Generosity created open doors for the gospel to be preached where it had never been heard before. Every evangelist needs a sender—and senders must be faithful sowers.

Scriptures:

- **"How shall they preach unless they are sent? As it is written: 'How beautiful are the feet of those who preach the gospel of peace…'" —Romans 10:15 (NKJV)**

- **"Moreover, as you Philippians know, in the early days of your acquaintance with the gospel… you sent me aid more than once when I was in need." —Philippians 4:15–16 (NIV)**

- **"The worker deserves his wages." —Luke 10:7 (NIV)**

Application: When you give, you don't just sow into buildings—you send messengers.

2. *Generosity Breaks Ground for Souls*

Just as farmers must invest seed in the soil before expecting a harvest, people of the kingdom must sow financial seed into

Money and the Harvest

evangelism before expecting souls to be saved. Generosity opens spiritual ground for the gospel to take root in hearts, especially in areas where people are unreached or impoverished.

Scriptures:

- **"Those who sow with tears will reap with songs of joy. Those who go out weeping, carrying seed to sow, will return with songs of joy, carrying sheaves with them."** —Psalm 126:5–6 (NKJV)

- **"Give, and it will be given to you... For with the measure you use, it will be measured to you."** —Luke 6:38 (NIV)

- **"Honor the Lord with your wealth... then your barns will be filled..."** —Proverbs 3:9–10 (NIV)

Application: The more we invest in the mission, the greater the harvest we can expect.

3. *Giving Makes the Gospel Visible*

Generosity demonstrates the love of God in tangible ways. Feeding the hungry, clothing the poor, and serving communities open hearts to the gospel. Many will receive Christ after they've seen His love in action. Generosity is evangelism in motion.

Scriptures:

- **"Let your light shine before others, that they may see your good deeds and glorify your Father in heaven."** —

Matthew 5:16 (NIV)

- "If anyone has material possessions and sees a brother or sister in need but has no pity on them, how can the love of God be in that person?" —1 John 3:17 (NIV)

- "Whatever you did for one of the least of these brothers and sisters of mine, you did for Me." —Matthew 25:40 (NIV)

Application: When people see the generosity of God through His people, they are more open to receiving the message of salvation.

4. *God Entrusts More to Those Who Give for His Glory*

When God finds someone who gives with a kingdom purpose—not for personal gain, but for soul-winning impact—He multiplies their resources. Why? Because they have become a channel, not a container. A generous believer becomes a trusted steward of revival.

Scriptures:

- "Now He who supplies seed to the sower and bread for food will also supply and increase your store of seed and will enlarge the harvest of your righteousness." —2 Corinthians 9:10 (NIV)

- "You will be enriched in every way so that you can be generous on every occasion, and through us your generosity will result in thanksgiving to God." —2 Corinthians 9:11 (NIV)

Money and the Harvest

- "But the one who does not know and does things deserving punishment will be beaten with few blows. From everyone who has been given much, much will be demanded; and from the one who has been entrusted with much, much more will be asked." —Luke 12:48 (NIV)

Application: If you make God's priority your priority, He will provide what you need to keep giving.

5. *The Great Commission Needs Great Provision*

Jesus gave the church the Great Commission—not the Great Suggestion. But we cannot fulfill it with words alone. It takes trained workers, strategic outreach, digital tools, transportation, discipleship resources, and, yes—financial investment.

Scriptures:

- "Therefore go and make disciples of all nations, baptizing them in the name of the Father and of the Son and of the Holy Spirit." —Matthew 28:19 (NIV)

- "The harvest is plentiful, but the workers are few. Ask the Lord of the harvest, therefore, to send out workers into his harvest field." —Luke 10:2 (NIV)

- "But how can they hear without someone preaching to them?" —Romans 10:14 (NIV)

If evangelism is the engine, then generosity is the fuel. One cannot operate without the other.

Pastor Dr. Claudine Benjamin

Your Generosity Preaches

Every time you give to evangelism, you preach the gospel. You may not hold a microphone, but your giving speaks louder than words. It declares: *"Souls matter. The gospel is urgent. And I am willing to fund heaven's agenda?"*

You may never go to the mission field—but your seed can.

You may never preach to thousands—but your giving can reach them.

You may not be the one harvesting—but your generosity makes it possible.

Evangelism without funding becomes limited and short-lived. But where there is generosity, the gospel moves freely, reaching people who may have never encountered Christ.

> **"He that hath a bountiful eye shall be blessed; for he giveth of his bread to the poor." —Proverbs 22:9 (KJV)**

> **"There is that scattereth, and yet increaseth…" —Proverbs 11:24 (KJV)**

Generosity spreads the gospel further and faster than any program ever could.

Giving Is an Act of Revival Worship

In times of true revival, giving is not a burden—it becomes an act of worship. The heart stirred by God longs to honor Him with substance.

"Honour the Lord with thy substance, and with the firstfruits of all thine increase." —Proverbs 3:9 (KJV)

The Macedonian church exemplified this in the New Testament. Even in great poverty, they gave generously:

"…in a great trial of affliction the abundance of their joy and their deep poverty abounded unto the riches of their liberality." —2 Corinthians 8:2 (KJV)

True revival releases joy that overflows into generosity.

Generosity Breaks Spiritual Strongholds

Generosity is far more than a financial transaction—it is a spiritual confrontation. Every time a believer gives sacrificially, they wage war against the powers of darkness that seek to keep them bound in fear, selfishness, and poverty. Generosity destroys the grip of Mammon, breaks the strongholds of poverty, and dethrones idols in the heart.

You cannot walk in kingdom freedom without embracing kingdom generosity.

1. Generosity Breaks the Stronghold of Greed

Greed is not always loud and obvious—it's subtle, seductive, and deeply rooted in self-preservation. It whispers, *"You don't have enough. You need to hold on to more."* Generosity silences that voice. When you give, especially when it costs you, you declare that God is your Source, not your possessions.

Scriptures:

- "Watch out! Be on your guard against all kinds of greed; life does not consist in an abundance of possessions." —Luke 12:15 (NIV)

- "You cannot serve both God and money." —Matthew 6:24 (NIV)

- "Command them to do good, to be rich in good deeds, and to be generous and willing to share." —1 Timothy 6:18 (NIV)

Application: Every act of generosity pulls down the idol of greed and declares trust in God, not stuff.

2. *Generosity Breaks the Stronghold of Fear*

Fear says, *"What if you don't have enough?"* But generosity says, *"I trust God to provide."* Fear causes people to hoard. Faith causes people to release. Every time you give, you break the spirit of fear that tries to convince you to keep everything for yourself.

Scriptures:

- "So do not worry, saying, 'What shall we eat?' or 'What shall we drink?'... But seek first His Kingdom... and all these things will be given to you." —Matthew 6:31–33 (NIV)

- "For the Spirit God gave us does not make us timid, but gives us power, love and self-discipline." —2 Timothy 1:7 (NKJV)

- **"There is no fear in love. But perfect love drives out fear…"** —1 John 4:18 (NIV)

Application: Giving is a declaration that your faith is bigger than your fear. It confronts anxiety and replaces it with peace.

3. Generosity Breaks the Stronghold of Pride and Self-Reliance

Some people don't give because they believe they are self-made. Pride says, *"I earned this. I built this. I deserve this."* But generosity humbles the heart and acknowledges God as the Giver of every good thing.

Scriptures:

- **"Remember the Lord your God, for it is He who gives you the ability to produce wealth…"** —Deuteronomy 8:18 (NIV)

- **"Every good and perfect gift is from above, coming down from the Father…"** —James 1:17 (NIV)

- **"God opposes the proud but shows favor to the humble."** —James 4:6 (NIV)

Application: When you give, you surrender your ego and exalt the One who gave you everything.

4. Generosity Breaks the Stronghold of Poverty Mindset

A poverty mindset believes there's never enough—it limits your vision, minimizes your faith, and paralyzes your obedience. But generosity declares that you live under kingdom supply, not earthly limitation. It shifts your focus from scarcity to abundance.

Scriptures:

- "The Lord is my shepherd, I lack nothing." —Psalm 23:1 (NIV)

- "Now to Him who is able to do immeasurably more than all we ask or imagine…" —Ephesians 3:20 (NIV)

- "You will be enriched in every way so that you can be generous on every occasion…" —2 Corinthians 9:11 (NIV)

Application: You don't give because you have a lot—you give because you know your God is not limited.

5. *Generosity Breaks the Stronghold of Stagnation and Barrenness*

When you stop giving, you stop flowing. Generosity keeps the spiritual waters of your life moving. It positions you for fresh outpouring, new breakthroughs, and divine favor. Stinginess leads to stagnation; giving releases multiplication.

Scriptures:

- "One person gives freely, yet gains even more; another withholds unduly, but comes to poverty." —Proverbs 11:24 (NIV)

Money and the Harvest

- "Give, and it will be given to you... For with the measure you use, it will be measured to you." —Luke 6:38 (NIV)

- "The generous will prosper; those who refresh others will themselves be refreshed." —Proverbs 11:25 (NLT)

Application: Giving isn't just an act—it's a breakthrough strategy. It triggers blessing, favor, and fruitfulness.

Giving Is Warfare

Generosity is more than kindness—it is spiritual warfare. Every dollar, every offering, every act of giving becomes a weapon in the hand of a believer. It tears down strongholds, builds up the kingdom, and declares that God—not mammon—is in control.

Your generosity breaks chains.

Your obedience releases favor.

Your sacrifice silences the enemy.

Greed, selfishness, and fear can block the flow of the Spirit. But when generosity is released, those strongholds are broken. Giving dismantles the hold of mammon and invites God's presence and provision.

> "Bring ye all the tithes into the storehouse... and prove me now herewith... if I will not open you the windows of heaven..." —Malachi 3:10 (KJV)

Pastor Dr. Claudine Benjamin

> **"Where your treasure is, there will your heart be also."** — **Matthew 6:21 (KJV)**

When we give, our hearts align with heaven. And when heaven's priorities become ours, revival becomes unstoppable.

When the Church Gives, the Fire Falls

The church must move beyond budget-based giving and into revival-driven giving. Revival cannot be contained in four walls—it must be resourced to spread into the streets, schools, cities, and nations.

> **"And all that believed were together, and had all things common... And the Lord added to the church daily such as should be saved." —Acts 2:44, 47 (KJV)**

The fire fell where unity and generosity met. God still responds to that pattern today.

Reflection Questions

1. Are you generous in a way that reflects revival fire?

2. Do you give out of obligation or out of joyful surrender?

3. Is your generosity fueling the gospel beyond your local church?

Prayer

Lord, ignite in me a spirit of radical generosity. Let my giving be a reflection of the revival I long to see. Break every spirit of fear, greed, and withholding in my life. Use me to fund the flames of revival so that many may come to know You. In Jesus' name. Amen.

Part 3

Breaking Financial Bondage for the Sake of the Harvest

Chapter 7

The Spirit of Mammon vs. the Spirit of God

There is a war raging in the hearts of believers—a war between the Spirit of God and the spirit of mammon. Mammon is not just another word for money; it is a spiritual force that seeks to rule and control people through fear, greed, and materialism. Jesus made it clear: you cannot serve both God and money. The church must choose—serve money or serve God. There is no middle ground.

What Is Mammon?

Mammon is a demonic spirit that attaches itself to money and seeks to dominate and deceive. It convinces people that money is the answer to their problems, that more money equals more power, and that possessions define identity.

> "**No man can serve two masters: for either he will hate the one, and love the other...Ye cannot serve God and mammon.**" —Matthew 6:24 (KJV)

Mammon seeks worship. It demands allegiance. It offers counterfeit security.

The Spirit of Mammon is Rooted in Fear and Pride

Mammon feeds on the fear of lack and pride in self-sufficiency. It whispers, *"You can't give that—what if you don't have enough?"* or *"You don't need God—you've got money."*

> **"The rich man's wealth is his strong city, and as a high wall in his own conceit." —Proverbs 18:11 (KJV)**

> **"They trust in their wealth, and boast themselves in the multitude of their riches." —Psalm 49:6 (KJV)**

This spirit seduces people into believing that money equals control, and, thus, they put their trust in riches instead of God.

The Spirit of God Brings Freedom and Generosity

In contrast, the Spirit of God invites us to live in faith, generosity, and full trust in the Father. Where mammon says, *"Keep,"* the Holy Spirit says, *"Give."* Where mammon says, *"You earned it,"* the Spirit reminds us, *"It was entrusted to you."*

> **"Now the Lord is that Spirit: and where the Spirit of the Lord is, there is liberty." —2 Corinthians 3:17 (KJV)**

> **"The liberal soul shall be made fat: and he that watereth shall be watered also himself." —Proverbs 11:25 (KJV)**

Where the Spirit of God is honored, people give freely—not under compulsion, but out of joy and obedience.

Mammon Opposes the Gospel

Mammon wants control. So, it opposes missions, tithing, giving, and anything that advances the kingdom. It whispers lies like:

- *"The church just wants your money."*
- *"You can't afford to give."*
- *"Let someone else support the mission."*

"The love of money is the root of all evil..." —1 Timothy 6:10 (KJV)

The spirit of mammon often hides behind religious excuses. But its fruit is always fear, selfishness, and withholding.

Discerning Which Spirit You Serve

Ask yourself:

- Does money control my decisions?
- Do I hesitate to give, even when God prompts me?
- Do I view money as a source instead of a resource?

"For where your treasure is, there will your heart be also." —Matthew 6:21 (KJV)

Your giving habits are a direct reflection of who is on the throne of your heart—God or mammon.

Breaking Agreement with Mammon

To break the power of mammon, you must repent, renounce, and replace. This is not just a mental shift—it is a spiritual warfare strategy to dethrone the influence of mammon from your heart and place God back on the throne as your Source.

1. Repent for Trusting Money Over God

Repentance is the first step to freedom. Mammon, a spirit that attaches itself to money, thrives when we begin to trust in our bank accounts, jobs, or material wealth more than we trust in Jehovah Jireh, our Provider.

Scriptures:

- **"No one can serve two masters. Either you will hate the one and love the other, or you will be devoted to the one and despise the other. You cannot serve both God and money." —Matthew 6:24 (NIV)**

- **"Those who trust in their riches will fall, but the righteous will thrive like a green leaf." —Proverbs 11:28 (NIV)**

- **"Some trust in chariots and some in horses, but we trust in the name of the Lord our God." —Psalm 20:7 (NIV)**

Application: Ask God to forgive you for misplaced trust and surrender control of your finances back to Him. Repentance is not just a prayer—it's a change of allegiance.

2. Renounce the Spirit of Mammon and Its Lies

Renunciation is the act of verbally and spiritually rejecting the authority of mammon in your life. Mammon lies by saying:

Money and the Harvest

- *"You don't have enough."*
- *"You are secure because of money."*
- *"You can't afford to give."*

These lies create fear, greed, and anxiety. Renounce them and declare God's truth instead.

Scriptures:

- **"For the love of money is a root of all kinds of evil. Some people, eager for money, have wandered from the faith and pierced themselves with many griefs." —1 Timothy 6:10 (NIV)**

- **"The thief comes only to steal and kill and destroy; I have come that they may have life, and have it to the full." —John 10:10 (NIV)**

- **"Submit yourselves, then, to God. Resist the devil, and he will flee from you." —James 4:7 (NIV)**

Application: Verbally reject mammon and every lie it has planted in your heart. Declare that your provision and identity come from God alone.

3. Replace It with Truth—Practice Giving, Tithing, and Kingdom Generosity

You cannot cast out mammon without replacing its influence. The practical antidote to mammon is generosity. Giving dethrones mammon and demonstrates trust in God's economy. Tithing and offering are not just obligations—they are declarations of faith.

Scriptures:

- "Bring the whole tithe into the storehouse, that there may be food in my house. Test me in this," says the Lord Almighty, "and see if I will not throw open the floodgates of heaven and pour out so much blessing that there will not be room enough to store it." —Malachi 3:10 (NIV)

- "Give, and it will be given to you. A good measure, pressed down, shaken together and running over, will be poured into your lap." —Luke 6:38 (NIV)

- "Each of you should give what you have decided in your heart to give, not reluctantly or under compulsion, for God loves a cheerful giver." —2 Corinthians 9:7 (NIV)

Make giving a lifestyle. Don't just give when it's convenient—give when it costs. Tithing, offering, blessing others, and funding missions are all ways to establish God's reign over your resources.

> "Charge them that are rich... that they be not high-minded, nor trust in uncertain riches, but in the living God..." —1 Timothy 6:17 (KJV)

Jesus broke the power of mammon when He taught us to trust God for our daily bread (see Matthew 6:11) and to seek the kingdom first (see Matthew 6:33).

You Can't Fund the Harvest While Serving Mammon

The spirit of mammon cripples the church's effectiveness. Revival, missions, and evangelism are often hindered not by a lack of vision but by a lack of surrendered provision.

Money and the Harvest

You cannot sow into the harvest while clutching your wallet in fear. You cannot serve two masters.

> **"And he said unto them, Take heed, and beware of covetousness…"** —Luke 12:15 (KJV)

The spirit of God leads to release. The spirit of mammon demands control. Choose this day whom you will serve.

Reflection Questions

1. Are you trusting God or trusting money?

2. Do you hold back from giving out of fear?

3. Have you unknowingly come into agreement with mammon?

Prayer

Father, I renounce every agreement I have made with the spirit of mammon. I declare that You alone are my Source and Sustainer. Break the power of fear and greed in my life. Fill me with the Holy Spirit, and make me a joyful giver. I choose to serve You, not mammon. In Jesus' name. Amen.

Chapter 8

Poverty, Prosperity, and Purpose

There is confusion in the body of Christ about money. Some preach a poverty gospel—equating holiness with a lack of material possessions—while others promote a prosperity gospel that equates godliness with financial abundance. But both extremes miss the heart of God. Biblical finance is about purpose—not poverty or indulgent prosperity. God blesses His people not so they can hoard wealth but so they can advance the kingdom and bless others.

Poverty Is Not Piety

There is no virtue in poverty for its own sake. While God calls us to humility and dependence on Him, He never glorifies a lack of resources as a spiritual standard.

> "The Lord is my shepherd; I shall not want." —Psalm 23:1 (KJV)

> "I have been young, and now am old; yet have I not seen the righteous forsaken, nor his seed begging bread." —Psalm 37:25 (KJV)

Poverty is often the result of broken systems, disobedience, or oppression—not divine calling. God delights in meeting the needs of His people.

Prosperity is Not Permission for Greed

God does bless His people, but prosperity without purpose becomes idolatry. Prosperity is a tool, not a trophy. It is never an end in itself.

> **"Charge them that are rich… that they be not high-minded, nor trust in uncertain riches, but in the living God…" —1 Timothy 6:17 (KJV)**

> **"Beware that thou forget not the Lord thy God… when thou hast eaten and art full, and hast built goodly houses…" —Deuteronomy 8:11–12 (KJV)**

Scripture warns us not to let blessings replace our dependency on God.

God Prospers with Purpose

Biblical prosperity is always tied to God's purpose. He blesses His people so they can be a blessing.

> **"And I will bless thee… and thou shalt be a blessing." — Genesis 12:2 (KJV)**

> **"But thou shalt remember the Lord thy God: for it is he that giveth thee power to get wealth, that he may establish his covenant…" —Deuteronomy 8:18 (KJV)**

God funds people He can trust to fund His mission.

Jesus Was Not Wealthy—But He Was Never in Lack

Jesus lived simply, but He was not poor in the way poverty is defined today. He had access to every resource needed for His ministry.

> "For ye know the grace of our Lord Jesus Christ, that, though he was rich, yet for your sakes he became poor…" —2 Corinthians 8:9 (KJV)

Even though He emptied Himself of heavenly riches, He never lacked what was needed to fulfill His mission—food, shelter, travel, or ministry support (see Luke 8:2–3, Matthew 17:27).

The Danger of Loving Money

The issue is not money itself—but loving it, trusting it, and being controlled by it. That's where both poverty and prosperity become traps.

> "For the love of money is the root of all evil…" —1 Timothy 6:10 (KJV)

> "No man can serve two masters…Ye cannot serve God and mammon." —Matthew 6:24 (KJV)

Money is a great servant but a terrible master. It must be submitted to God's purpose.

Kingdom Wealth is Always Missional

The wealth God releases into your hands is meant to:

- Feed the poor

   "He that hath pity upon the poor lendeth unto the Lord..." —Proverbs 19:17 (KJV)

- Support ministry

   "Even so hath the Lord ordained that they which preach the gospel should live of the gospel." —1 Corinthians 9:14 (KJV)

- Advance the gospel

   "And how shall they preach, except they be sent?" —Romans 10:15 (KJV)

- Build generational blessing

   "A good man leaveth an inheritance to his children's children..." —Proverbs 13:22 (KJV)

When you see wealth through a kingdom lens, you manage it for mission, not for ego or excess.

God Wants You Whole—Spiritually and Financially

God is not just interested in saving your soul—He wants to bless the entirety of your life. That includes your finances.

"Beloved, I wish above all things that thou mayest prosper and be in health, even as thy soul prospereth." —3 John 1:2 (KJV)

When your soul prospers, your finances align with God's will. Prosperity with purpose leads to holiness, not selfishness.

Reflection Questions

1. Do you believe that money is a tool for God's purpose?

2. Have you embraced any wrong beliefs about poverty or prosperity?

3. Are you using what God gives you to impact others?

Prayer

Lord, I surrender my thinking about money. Break every false mindset of poverty and every deceptive pursuit of prosperity without purpose. Teach me to steward Your resources with wisdom, humility, and kingdom vision. Prosper me to fulfill Your calling on my life and to bless others. In Jesus' name. Amen.

Chapter 9

Debt, Distraction, and Delay in the Harvest

The enemy knows he cannot stop the harvest, but he will do everything he can to delay it. One of his most effective tools is financial bondage. Debt, unchecked distractions, and misplaced priorities have kept many believers and churches from fully stepping into their calling. When the people of God are burdened financially, mentally distracted, and spiritually delayed, the harvest suffers.

Debt is a Spiritual Weight

Debt is not just a financial issue—it is a spiritual hindrance. It creates pressure and anxiety and often leads to compromise. It limits your ability to give, serve, and move when God says, "Go."

"the borrower is servant to the lender." —Proverbs 22:7 (KJV)

When we are in debt, our decisions are often controlled by our creditors rather than our own calling. That's not freedom—it's bondage.

Debt Prevents Kingdom Investment

Many Christians desire to give, but they cannot because of credit card debt, loans, and other forms of consumer debt. Debt redirects finances from kingdom purposes to worldly interest payments.

> **"Owe no man any thing, but to love one another…" — Romans 13:8 (KJV)**

God's desire is not only to bless us but to free us so we can bless others and fund the gospel without restriction.

Distraction Diminishes Kingdom Focus

Beyond debt, the enemy uses distraction—endless financial pursuits, materialism, side hustles, and get-rich schemes—to pull believers away from the harvest.

> **"And the cares of this world, and the deceitfulness of riches, and the lusts of other things entering in, choke the word, and it becometh unfruitful." —Mark 4:19 (KJV)**

We must ask: Are we busy with work and wealth but idle in kingdom purposes? Distraction often masks itself as diligence—but it diverts us from divine assignment.

Delayed Obedience Is Disobedience

When God says "give," "go," or "build," but we delay due to finances, we're not just being cautious—we're being disobedient. Delay in action is often the result of a lack of preparation or misplaced trust.

> "He that observeth the wind shall not sow; and he that regardeth the clouds shall not reap." —Ecclesiastes 11:4 (KJV)

If you wait for the "perfect financial moment" to obey God, you'll miss the harvest. Faith acts even when the bank account doesn't look ready.

Budgeting for the Harvest

If we are serious about winning souls, planting churches, sending missionaries, and funding end-time revival, we must take budgeting seriously. Budgeting for the harvest involves aligning your personal and ministry finances with God's mission. It is the intentional act of stewarding resources with eternity in mind.

Many believers want to be generous but struggle to give consistently or sacrificially due to poor financial planning. Vision without discipline leads to frustration. But when vision meets structure—impact happens.

1. Stewardship is the Foundation of Revival Finance

God doesn't bless mismanagement. He blesses faithful stewardship. Budgeting is a spiritual discipline that honors God by placing Him first, tracking what He provides, and planning how to invest it in what matters most—souls.

Scriptures:

- "Moreover, it is required of stewards that they be found faithful." —1 Corinthians 4:2 (ESV)

- "Be sure you know the condition of your flocks, give careful attention to your herds; for riches do not endure forever..." —Proverbs 27:23–24 (NIV)

- "Suppose one of you wants to build a tower. Won't you first sit down and estimate the cost to see if you have enough money to complete it?" —Luke 14:28 (NIV)

Application: Stewardship without strategy is incomplete. Budgeting is how we put stewardship into action.

2. Create a Kingdom-Focused Budget

A harvest-minded budget is not just about bills, savings, and leisure—it's about assigning resources to God's priorities. Your budget should reflect your commitment to:

- Tithing and offerings
- Giving to missions and outreach
- Supporting evangelism efforts
- Investing in your local church
- Reserving seed for spontaneous kingdom opportunities

Scriptures:

- "Honor the Lord with your wealth, with the firstfruits of all your crops." —Proverbs 3:9 (NIV)

- "Each of you should give what you have decided in your heart to give..." —2 Corinthians 9:7 (NIV)

- "Give to everyone who asks you, and if anyone takes what belongs to you, do not demand it back." —Luke 6:30 (NIV)

Application: Your budget should tell the story of your faith, priorities, and obedience.

3. *Eliminate Waste to Empower Giving*

Many times, we want to give more, but we can't—because too much is wasted. Subscriptions, impulsive spending, disorganization, and lack of planning can choke your ability to give. When we remove financial waste, we free up space for kingdom impact.

Scriptures:

- "The wise store up choice food and olive oil, but fools gulp theirs down." —Proverbs 21:20 (NIV)

- "Gather the pieces that are left over. Let nothing be wasted." —John 6:12 (NIV)

- "Go to the ant… it stores its provisions in summer and gathers its food at harvest." —Proverbs 6:6–8 (NIV)

Application: Every dollar you redirect from waste can become a seed in the harvest field.

4. *Prepare for the Unexpected Harvest*

Sometimes God sends unexpected opportunities to sow into missions, help a hurting family, or fund an evangelistic event. When you've budgeted in advance, you're ready to respond. Budgeting gives you a margin for obedience.

Scriptures:

- "Be ready in season and out of season..." —**2 Timothy 4:2 (NKJV)**

- "Joseph stored up huge quantities of grain... so that the country would not be ruined by the famine." —**Genesis 41:48, 36 (NIV)**

- "The plans of the diligent lead surely to abundance..." —**Proverbs 21:5 (ESV)**

Application: A harvest is often time-sensitive. If your finances are ready, you can move with the Spirit and not miss the moment.

5. *Budgeting Helps You Build for the Long-Term Mission*

Revival is not a one-time event—it is a long-term movement. Budgeting allows churches and individuals to plan ahead, fund future projects, and expand their reach. Whether it's a church plant, a missions trip, a media campaign, or community evangelism—vision needs funding with foresight.

Scriptures:

- "Write the vision and make it plain on tablets, that he may run who reads it." —**Habakkuk 2:2 (NKJV)**

- "Through [skillful and godly] wisdom a house [a life, a home, a family] is built, and by understanding it is established [on a sound and good foundation]" — Proverbs 24:3 (AMP)

- **"The prudent see danger and take refuge, but the simple keep going and pay the penalty." —Proverbs 22:3 (NIV)**

Don't just pray for provision—prepare for it. Budgeting aligns your vision with heaven's strategy.

Budget with the Harvest in Mind

God gives seed to the sower, but if the sower has no plan, the seed may be lost. Budgeting for the harvest is about assigning purpose to your provision. It's a declaration that says, *"My money serves the mission. My resources are for revival. My budget is built for souls."*

You don't need more money to make an impact—you need more mission in your money.

One practical way to avoid debt, distraction, and delay is by budgeting with the kingdom in mind. Many believers budget for bills and desires but leave nothing for the gospel.

> **"Prepare thy work without, and make it fit for thyself in the field; and afterwards build thine house." —Proverbs 24:27 (KJV)**

A kingdom budget prioritizes giving, sowing, and fulfilling divine assignments. It makes room for obedience, not just comfort.

Pastor Dr. Claudine Benjamin

Freedom from Financial Bondage Unlocks Harvest Potential

When believers break free from debt and distractions, they become powerful vessels for the harvest. Financial freedom allows you to give, move, and respond without hesitation.

> **"Stand fast therefore in the liberty wherewith Christ hath made us free…" —Galatians 5:1 (KJV)**

God is not just interested in financial increase—He desires your financial freedom so you can be a harvest laborer unhindered by worldly constraints.

The Harvest Waits for a Free Church

The harvest is plentiful, but the laborers are few (see Matthew 9:37). One reason? Too many laborers are bound by financial chains.

> **"Not slothful in business; fervent in spirit; serving the Lord." —Romans 12:11 (KJV)**

The church must rise above the weight of debt and the distractions of materialism to answer the call of the harvest with urgency and readiness.

Reflection Questions

1. Are you carrying debt that limits your ability to give or go?

2. Have you been more distracted by financial pursuits than by kingdom purpose?

3. What can you do today to start budgeting with the harvest in mind?

Prayer

Lord, deliver me from every financial burden that delays my obedience to You. Break the chains of debt, destroy every distraction, and give me clarity of purpose. Help me to prioritize Your kingdom in my finances, schedule, and life. I declare that I will not delay the harvest any longer. In Jesus' name. Amen.

Part 4

Becoming a Harvest Financier

Chapter 10

You Are God's Banker

God is raising up a people who understand that they are not just believers—they are kingdom financiers. You are not simply called to accumulate wealth but to manage divine resources for eternal purposes. As a kingdom banker, your assignment is to receive, steward, and release what God entrusts to you in alignment with His will for the harvest.

God Entrusts Resources, Not Just Blessings

Many believers seek blessings from God, but far fewer understand that blessing comes with responsibility. God does not simply bless us to make our lives easier—He entrusts us with resources to advance His kingdom on earth. The difference between a consumer and a steward is the understanding that what I have is not mine—it's been entrusted to me by God.

God is not just looking for people to bless—He's looking for people to trust.

1. **Blessings Are Meant to Flow Through You, Not Just to You**

God's economy operates on the principle of flow. When He gives, He expects that what's in your hand will be used to bless others, advance the gospel, and glorify Him. If you hoard what God gives, it can become a curse instead of a blessing.

Scripture:

- "I will bless you…and you will be a blessing…All peoples on earth will be blessed through you." —Genesis 12:2–3 (NIV)

- "…Freely you have received; freely give." —Matthew 10:8 (NIV)

- "…From everyone who has been given much, much will be demanded…" —Luke 12:48 (NIV)

Application: Ask yourself, *"What have I received that God wants to use for others?"*

2. Resources Are Assignments, Not Just Assets

The money, influence, connections, and open doors you've received are not just assets for your enjoyment—they are assignments for kingdom fulfillment. When God gives you more, it's not just to elevate your lifestyle—it's to expand your impact.

Scriptures:

- "The earth is the Lord's, and everything in it, the world, and all who live in it." —Psalm 24:1 (NIV)

- "As each has received a gift, use it to serve one another, as good stewards of God's varied grace." —1 Peter 4:10 (ESV)

- "You may say to yourself, 'My power... have produced this wealth for me.' But remember the Lord your God, for it is He who gives you the ability to produce wealth..." —Deuteronomy 8:17–18 (NIV)

Application: What you've been given comes with heaven's purpose attached. Don't just manage it—multiply it.

3. Faithfulness Determines Future Entrustment

God measures trustworthiness not by how much you desire but by how well you manage what you already have. If you're faithful with the little, God can entrust you with more—not for hoarding, but for kingdom building.

Scriptures:

- "You have been faithful with a few things; I will put you in charge of many things." —Matthew 25:23 (NIV)

- "So if you have not been trustworthy in handling worldly wealth, who will trust you with true riches?" —Luke 16:11 (NIV)

- "Well done, good and faithful servant!" —Matthew 25:21 (NIV)

You don't qualify for increase by asking—you qualify by stewarding.

4. Resources Are Tools to Fund God's Agenda

Your resources were never meant to serve only personal goals. They are tools in the hand of a yielded believer to fuel evangelism, discipleship, missions, outreach, and compassion. Your job, business, and income are part of God's supply chain for the expansion of the kingdom.

Scriptures:

- "Each of you should give… not reluctantly or under compulsion, for God loves a cheerful giver." —2 Corinthians 9:7 (NIV)

- "Bring the whole tithe into the storehouse… and see if I will not… pour out so much blessing…" —Malachi 3:10 (NIV)

- "And how can anyone preach unless they are sent?" —Romans 10:15 (NIV)

Application: Your provision is connected to your purpose—don't separate the two.

5. God Doesn't Entrust Where He Can't Trust

If you want to receive more from God, ask: *Can He trust me with what I already have?* God looks for vessels who will not leak His glory, misuse His provision, or idolize the gift. Integrity, obedience, and spiritual alignment are required to be entrusted with divine resources.

Scriptures:

- "Who then is the faithful and wise servant… whom the master has put in charge of the servants?" —Matthew 24:45 (NIV)

Money and the Harvest

- "If you are faithful in little things, you will be faithful in large ones." —Luke 16:10 (NLT)

- "But he gives us more grace." —James 4:6 (NIV)

Application: The question is not whether God will give it. But can you be trusted to handle it?

You Are Not Just Blessed—You Are Entrusted

To live as a kingdom steward is to shift your mindset from one of ownership to one of management. What's in your hand belongs to the King. What's in your account has kingdom assignment. What's in your possession is heaven's provision—for someone else's transformation.

You are not just blessed—you are entrusted.

You are not just called—you are commissioned.

You are not just a receiver—you are a releaser.

Everything you have—finances, talents, influence—is not just a blessing to enjoy but a trust to manage. God doesn't randomly bless; He strategically entrusts resources to those He can use for kingdom impact.

> "Moreover it is required in stewards, that a man be found faithful." —1 Corinthians 4:2 (KJV)

> "The silver is mine, and the gold is mine, saith the Lord of hosts." —Haggai 2:8 (KJV)

God is not looking for owners—He's looking for stewards. He puts His wealth in the hands of those who will release it for His work.

Bankers Don't Hoard—They Circulate Resources

The role of a banker is to distribute and manage funds, not to hoard them. Likewise, you are called to circulate kingdom wealth—releasing it to missions, ministries, and people in need.

> **"He that hath a bountiful eye shall be blessed; for he giveth of his bread to the poor." —Proverbs 22:9 (KJV)**

> **"…Freely ye have received, freely give." —Matthew 10:8 (KJV)**

Every time you give according to God's prompting, you're acting as a spiritual banker—releasing heaven's agenda on earth.

Faithfulness Unlocks Greater Assignments

Jesus taught that those who are faithful with little will be trusted with much more. If God can trust you to steward what you have now, He will increase your capacity.

> **"…thou hast been faithful over a few things, I will make thee ruler over many things…" —Matthew 25:21 (KJV)**

The more you obey with what you have, the more God will entrust to you—not for self-gain, but for greater harvest impact.

You Represent the Kingdom's Interests

Just as earthly bankers represent the interests of a financial institution, you represent heaven's priorities on the earth. Your financial decisions have eternal consequences.

> **"Lay not up for yourselves treasures upon earth... But lay up for yourselves treasures in heaven..." —Matthew 6:19–20 (KJV)**

Your giving builds churches, feeds the hungry, trains leaders, and saves souls. That's more than generosity—it's divine banking.

Biblical Examples of Kingdom Bankers

- Joseph of Arimathea used his wealth to bury Jesus honorably (see Matthew 27:57–60).
- Lydia, a wealthy businesswoman, hosted the church in her home (see Acts 16:14–15).
- The women who followed Jesus used their means to support His ministry (see Luke 8:1–3).
- Barnabas, full of the Holy Spirit, sold land and gave the money for kingdom use (see Acts 4:36–37).

These were not just givers—they were divinely appointed bankers of kingdom finance.

God is Looking for Distribution Centers

God is searching for men and women who will act as distribution centers—people who won't build bigger barns for themselves but will fund the work of the Lord without hesitation.

Pastor Dr. Claudine Benjamin

> **"But God said unto him, Thou fool, this night thy soul shall be required of thee: then whose shall those things be…?"**
> **—Luke 12:20 (KJV)**

You are not here to build your own empire—you are called to advance God's eternal kingdom.

Heaven Backs Kingdom Bankers

When you step into the role of a kingdom banker, heaven supports you. Divine provision follows divine purpose. You will see God multiply your seed—not just for you, but for the sake of souls.

> **"Now he that ministereth seed to the sower both minister bread for your food, and multiply your seed sown…"** **—2 Corinthians 9:10 (KJV)**

God gives seed to the sower, not the hoarder. If your heart is to give, God will supply.

Reflection Questions

1. Do you see yourself as a manager of God's resources?
2. Are you actively distributing what He entrusts to you?
3. Can God trust you to finance the harvest?

Prayer

Father, I recognize that everything I have belongs to You. Make me a faithful kingdom banker—one who receives with humility, manages with integrity, and gives with generosity. I surrender my finances to Your will. Use me to fund the gospel, bless the poor, and equip the church. In Jesus' name. Amen.

Chapter 11

Sowing Seeds That Reap Souls

Every seed sown into God's kingdom has an eternal impact. When you give financially to soul-winning efforts, you are not just helping an organization—you are planting a spiritual seed into the soil of salvation. Souls are the greatest harvest in heaven, and giving toward that cause is one of the most powerful investments a believer can make. You may never stand on a stage or preach a sermon—but your seed can go where you cannot.

Giving is Spiritual Sowing

Scripture likens giving to planting seed. When you sow into good ground, you activate spiritual laws that produce supernatural results.

> **"But this I say, He which soweth sparingly shall reap also sparingly; and he which soweth bountifully shall reap also bountifully." —2 Corinthians 9:6 (KJV)**

> **"Be not deceived; God is not mocked: for whatsoever a man soweth, that shall he also reap." —Galatians 6:7 (KJV)**

Your giving today is a seed that bears fruit tomorrow—sometimes on earth, always in eternity.

Pastor Dr. Claudine Benjamin

Sowing into Souls is Heaven's Priority

In heaven's economy, the greatest investment is not in land, buildings, or assets—it is in souls. While the world measures value by profit, heaven measures value by people. The most important harvest field is not the stock market, real estate, or retirement accounts—it is the eternal souls of men and women.

Every time you give to the work of the gospel—evangelism, missions, church planting, and discipleship—you are sowing into what God prioritizes most. Souls are heaven's treasure, and when you invest in them, you are participating in God's eternal agenda.

1. Souls Are the Currency of Heaven

Heaven rejoices over one sinner who repents. Angels don't celebrate buildings, budgets, or status—they rejoice over souls. That's where God's heart is. When you sow into evangelism, you partner with heaven's mission.

Scriptures:

- **"...there is rejoicing in the presence of the angels of God over one sinner who repents." —Luke 15:10 (NIV)**

- **"For the Son of Man came to seek and to save the lost." —Luke 19:10 (NIV)**

- **"...he who wins souls is wise." —Proverbs 11:30 (NKJV)**

Application: If it causes heaven to rejoice, it should compel us to give.

2. The Seed You Sow Funds the Souls You Reach

Soul winning requires resources. Gospel campaigns, tracts, mission trips, digital evangelism, church outreaches—all cost money. Your giving provides the tools that make salvation accessible to those who might never hear otherwise.

Scriptures:

- "...how can they hear without someone preaching to them? And how can anyone preach unless they are sent?" —Romans 10:14–15 (NIV)

- "Give, and it will be given to you... For with the measure you use, it will be measured to you." —Luke 6:38 (NIV)

- "Those who sow in tears shall reap in joy." —Psalm 126:5 (NKJV)

Application: Every dollar you sow becomes a seed in someone's salvation story.

3. Sowing into Souls Is an Eternal Investment

Earthly investments fade. Markets crash. Possessions pass away. But every soul saved is a forever reward. When you give to the cause of Christ, you're storing up treasures in heaven that cannot be stolen, lost, or devalued.

Scriptures:

- "Do not store up for yourselves treasures on earth... But store up for yourselves treasures in heaven..." —

Matthew 6:19–20 (NIV)

- "The fruit of the righteous is a tree of life, and he who wins souls is wise." —Proverbs 11:30 (NKJV)

- "…each one's work will become manifest… and the fire will test what sort of work each one has done." —1 Corinthians 3:13 (ESV)

Application: What you give toward the gospel now echoes in eternity forever.

4. Sowing into Souls Aligns You with God's Heart

God is not just a Provider—He is a Pursuer of people. When you financially support soul-winning efforts, you are walking in sync with His heartbeat. You begin to see your resources as a tool to rescue, redeem, and restore lives.

Scriptures:

- "God so loved the world that He gave…" —John 3:16 (NIV)

- "The Lord is not slack concerning his promise, as some men count slackness; but is longsuffering to us-ward, not willing that any should perish, but that all should come to repentance." —2 Peter 3:9 (KJV)

- "Carry each other's burdens, and in this way you will fulfill the law of Christ." —Galatians 6:2 (NIV)

Money and the Harvest

Application: Giving to reach souls is not a donation—it's an imitation of God's love.

5. The Harvest Is Ripe—But It Needs Resources

Jesus declared that the harvest is plentiful, but the laborers are few. Laborers need to be equipped. Ministries need to be funded. Missions need to be sent. Your seed activates the harvest when you invest it into fertile ground—evangelism.

Scriptures:

- **"The harvest is plentiful, but the workers are few." — Luke 10:2 (NIV)**

- **"Honor the Lord with your wealth… then your barns will be filled…" —Proverbs 3:9–10 (NIV)**

- **"…whoever sows generously will also reap generously." —2 Corinthians 9:6 (NIV)**

The gospel is free, but sharing it with the lost requires faith, obedience, and financial support.

Give Where God's Heart Is

Heaven's priority is clear: saving souls, changing lives, and reaching nations. When you sow into souls, you are aligning your giving with God's highest agenda. There is no greater return, no deeper joy, and no higher calling.

Sow into souls—and you sow into eternity.

Give to reach the lost—and you give God your heart.

Invest in the gospel—and you invest in what matters most.

There is no greater soil than the salvation of souls. God's heart beats for the lost, and when you give to reach them, you touch the heart of God.

> **"The fruit of the righteous is a tree of life; and he that winneth souls is wise." —Proverbs 11:30 (KJV)**

> **"Likewise, I say unto you, there is joy in the presence of the angels of God over one sinner that repenteth." —Luke 15:10 (KJV)**

Heaven rejoices over one soul—and your seed can be the catalyst that brings them to Christ.

Every Seed Has a Story

You may never see the faces or hear the testimonies, but every soul won through your giving is part of your spiritual legacy. God keeps records of every righteous act—including financial generosity.

> **"Not because I desire a gift: but I desire fruit that may abound to your account." —Philippians 4:17 (KJV)**

Paul assured the Philippians that their giving produced spiritual fruit. Your giving is recorded, remembered, and rewarded by God.

The Law of Multiplication

God doesn't just return what you give—He multiplies it. This principle isn't about giving to get—it's about giving to grow the harvest.

Money and the Harvest

> **"Give, and it shall be given unto you; good measure, pressed down, and shaken together, and running over…"**
> **—Luke 6:38 (KJV)**

> **"He that ministereth seed to the sower… multiply your seed sown, and increase the fruits of your righteousness." —2 Corinthians 9:10 (KJV)**

When you sow into the gospel, you can expect a multiplied return—not just in your life, but in lives changed for eternity.

Don't Eat the Seed—Plant It

One of the enemy's greatest tricks is convincing believers to consume what God intended for sowing. If you eat your seed, you abort your harvest.

> **"There is that scattereth, and yet increaseth; and there is that withholdeth more than is meet, but it tendeth to poverty." —Proverbs 11:24 (KJV)**

You were never meant to hoard seed—you were born to release it into the soil of God's will.

Where You Sow Matters

Not all ground produces equally. You must discern where to sow—into ministries, missions, and outreaches that are actively winning souls and preaching the uncompromised gospel.

> **"But other fell into good ground, and brought forth fruit, some an hundredfold, some sixtyfold, some thirtyfold." — Matthew 13:8 (KJV)**

Pastor Dr. Claudine Benjamin

When you sow into good ground, you can expect a kingdom harvest that multiplies far beyond your natural effort.

Your Seed Goes Where You Can't

You may never travel to distant nations or preach in a revival meeting, but your financial seed can. When you give, you become a silent missionary—present in every soul reached, every hand raised, every baptism performed.

> **"And how shall they preach, except they be sent?" — Romans 10:15 (KJV)**

Senders are just as vital as goers. And in God's eyes, both share in the harvest.

Reflection Questions

1. Are you sowing financial seeds into soul-winning efforts?

2. Have you viewed your giving as an act of evangelism?

3. Are you expecting a spiritual return from the seeds you plant?

Prayer

Lord, thank You for giving me seed to sow. Help me to recognize the power and purpose of my giving. I commit to sow into good ground and support the preaching of the gospel. Let my seed bring forth a harvest of souls. Use my resources to expand Your kingdom and bring You glory. In Jesus' name. Amen.

Chapter 12

Strategic Giving for Strategic Harvests

Not all giving is equal in impact. While God honors every act of generosity, strategic giving—guided by purpose, prayer, and discernment—leads to strategic harvests. To reach the lost effectively, the church must shift from random generosity to intentional investment. It's time to fund what matters most: souls.

Strategic Giving Starts with Vision

Strategic givers don't give emotionally—they give intentionally. They don't just ask, *"What can I give?"* but *"Where will my giving make the most eternal difference?"*

"Where there is no vision, the people perish..." —Proverbs 29:18 (KJV)

Without a kingdom vision, giving becomes scattered and unfruitful. But when vision leads to giving, the impact is multiplied.

Ask God Where to Sow

Generosity without direction can lead to frustration. Giving without discernment can lead to loss. As kingdom stewards, we must understand that not every soil is good soil. While we are called to be generous, we are also called to be strategic—and the only way to give strategically is to ask God where to sow.

God knows where your seed will have the greatest impact. He knows which ministries are bearing fruit, which leaders are walking in integrity, and which harvest fields are ready. Before you release your resources, pause and pray: *"Lord, where is the ground You've assigned to me?"*

1. Not Every Need Is Your Assignment

The world is full of needs—but not every need is your seed ground. God has not called you to meet every need, but He has called you to meet the ones He directs you to. Spirit-led giving means you don't just respond to emotion—you respond to His instruction.

Scriptures:

- **"The steps of a good man are ordered by the Lord…" —Psalm 37:23 (KJV)**

- **"There is a way that seems right to a man, but its end is the way of death." —Proverbs 14:12 (NKJV)**

- **"Trust in the Lord with all your heart and lean not on your own understanding…" —Proverbs 3:5–6 (NIV)**

Application: Before you sow, seek—God will highlight your harvest field.

2. Your Seed Carries Kingdom Assignment

Money and the Harvest

Every seed God gives you is a tool for impact. But the assignment of that seed is tied to a specific place, person, or purpose. When you ask God where to sow, you align your giving with heaven's agenda, not just your personal preference.

Scriptures:

- **"…he who supplies seed to the sower and bread for food will also supply and increase your store of seed…" —2 Corinthians 9:10 (NIV)**

- **"For David… served the purpose of God in his own generation." —Acts 13:36 (ESV)**

- **"Whatever He says to you, do it." —John 2:5 (NKJV)**

Application: Don't waste strategic seed on unassigned soil. Ask the Holy Spirit for clarity.

3. God Honors Obedient Sowing More Than Impressive Sowing

It's not the amount you give but the obedience in how you give that unlocks supernatural harvest. God may tell you to sow into a small ministry, an unknown missionary, or a quiet servant of God—and your obedience will trigger uncommon favor.

Scriptures:

- **"To obey is better than sacrifice…" —1 Samuel 15:22 (NIV)**

- **"By faith Abel brought God a better offering than Cain did. By faith he was commended as righteous, when**

God spoke well of his offerings. And by faith Abel still speaks, even though he is dead." —Hebrews 11:4 (NIV)

- **"Wherever your treasure is, there the desires of your heart will also be." —Matthew 6:21 (NLT)**

Application: When you sow where God leads, you partner with heaven's exact blueprint.

4. Good Soil Produces Supernatural Return

Jesus taught us to sow into good ground—not just visible ground. Good soil is fruitful, faithful, and kingdom-aligned. When you ask God where to sow, you avoid shallow soil and discover places of maximum multiplication.

Scriptures:

- **"Still other seed fell on good soil. It came up, grew and produced a crop, some multiplying thirty, some sixty, some a hundred times" —Mark 4:8 (NIV)**

- **"You will be enriched in every way so that you can be generous on every occasion…" —2 Corinthians 9:11 (NIV)**

- **"Blessed is the one… whose delight is in the law of the Lord… whatever they do prospers." —Psalm 1:1–3 (NIV)**

Application: The right ground doesn't always look impressive—but it will produce divine results.

5. Prophetic Giving Unlocks Prophetic Harvest

Money and the Harvest

When you ask God where to sow, He may lead you to give prophetically—before the need arises or before the opportunity seems obvious. Spirit-led sowing is often a precursor to supernatural doors. What looks like sacrifice in the natural becomes strategy in the Spirit.

Scriptures:

- **"a woman came to him with an alabaster jar of very expensive perfume, which she poured on his head as he was reclining at the table." —Matthew 26:7 (NIV)**

- **"By faith Noah... built an ark to save his family." — Hebrews 11:7 (NIV)**

- **"Elijah said to her, 'Don't be afraid....first make a small loaf of bread for me...'" —1 Kings 17:13–14 (NIV)**

God may lead you to sow ahead of a harvest you haven't seen yet—but it's on the way.

Where You Sow Matters

Sowing into just any ground may bring temporary satisfaction—but sowing where God tells you brings eternal reward. The most powerful giving isn't random—it's revelational. As you seek the Lord about where to place your seed, He will lead you into divine partnerships, hidden harvests, and supernatural provision.

Don't just sow out of habit—sow by instruction.

Don't just give from emotion—give by revelation.

Pastor Dr. Claudine Benjamin

Ask God where to sow—and watch the kingdom explode through your obedience.

The most powerful giving decisions are made in prayer, not pressure. God knows where the need is, where the harvest is ripe, and where your seed is most needed.

> **"Trust in the Lord with all thine heart… and he shall direct thy paths." —Proverbs 3:5–6 (KJV)**

> **"If any of you lack wisdom, let him ask of God… and it shall be given him." —James 1:5 (KJV)**

Before you sow, ask heaven where to invest. Strategic giving begins with spiritual discernment.

Support the Front Lines

Those preaching the gospel, planting churches, and reaching the unreached should be top priorities for financial support.

> **"And how shall they preach, except they be sent?" — Romans 10:15 (KJV)**

Paul celebrated churches like the Philippians because they gave not just once but consistently to support gospel advancement (see Philippians 4:15–18). Strategic sowers sustain strategic movements.

Give Where the Gospel Is Going Forth

Not every cause, conference, or campaign is reaching the lost. Strategic givers must evaluate:

- Is this ministry winning souls?
- Are lives being transformed?
- Does this align with the great commission?

"Beloved, believe not every spirit, but try the spirits whether they are of God…" —1 John 4:1 (KJV)

"Ye shall know them by their fruits…" —Matthew 7:16 (KJV)

Check the fruit. Where you sow determines what kind of harvest you'll reap.

Fund the Future—Not Just the Familiar

It's easy to give where you've always given. But sometimes, God calls you to stretch and invest in new fields—emerging ministries, next-generation leaders, or unreached regions.

"Enlarge the place of thy tent… spare not, lengthen thy cords, and strengthen thy stakes." —Isaiah 54:2 (KJV)

Strategic giving involves taking a risk, not just repeating a routine. When God leads you beyond your comfort zone, there's always a greater harvest ahead.

Reallocate to What Matters Most

Many budgets are bloated with comforts but void of kingdom priorities. It's time to reallocate. Cancel what doesn't feed purpose. Fund what fuels purpose.

> "But seek ye first the kingdom of God, and his righteousness…" —Matthew 6:33 (KJV)

When the kingdom becomes your first investment, everything else aligns. You can't fund everything—but you can fund what God values most: souls.

Expect Results When You Sow in Obedience

Strategic giving isn't about calculation—it's about obedience and expectation. When you sow into God's work, you should expect to see results—not just in your life, but in the world.

> "…he which soweth bountifully shall reap also bountifully." —2 Corinthians 9:6 (KJV)

> "Thou shalt surely give him… because that for this thing the Lord thy God shall bless thee in all thy works…" — Deuteronomy 15:10 (KJV)

You're not giving to manipulate God—you're giving because you trust Him to produce eternal returns.

Strategic Giving Builds Generational Impact

What you fund today echoes into tomorrow. Souls saved today become evangelists tomorrow. Ministries launched now build disciples for decades. Your seed leaves a legacy.

> "A good man leaveth an inheritance to his children's children…" —Proverbs 13:22 (KJV)

"and thy seed shall possess the gate of his enemies." — Genesis 22:17 (KJV)

Strategic sowers don't just think in moments—they think in generations.

Reflection Questions

1. Have you prayed about where to sow your financial seed?

2. Are you funding what matters most to God?

3. What can you reallocate to make room for kingdom giving?

Prayer

Lord, make me a strategic sower. Give me vision to see where You are moving and wisdom to know where to plant my seed. Let me not give out of habit but out of purpose. Use my finances to fund the gospel, reach the lost, and build a lasting kingdom legacy. In Jesus' name. Amen.

Part 5

A Call to Harvest Partnership

Chapter 13

The Anointing of the Harvest Sponsor

There is a distinct anointing in the kingdom of God for those who are called to sponsor the harvest. These are not just generous givers—they are prophetic investors, entrusted with divine wealth to advance God's mission. When God places the burden of the harvest on a person's heart and gives them the resources to fulfill it, they carry a holy assignment: to fund, fuel, and finance the movement of the gospel on earth.

God Is Raising Up Kingdom Sponsors

Throughout scripture, we see individuals who were strategically placed and financially empowered to support God's work.

> **"And Joanna the wife of Chuza Herod's steward, and Susanna, and many others, which ministered unto him of their substance." —Luke 8:3 (KJV)**

These women funded Jesus' ministry. They were not just supporters—they were spirit-led harvest sponsors. God is still raising up people like them today.

The Sponsor's Anointing Requires Stewardship and Sensitivity

To be a sponsor in the kingdom, you must walk in both financial wisdom and spiritual discernment. God will entrust more to those who use what they already have for eternal purposes.

> **"If therefore ye have not been faithful in the unrighteous mammon, who will commit to your trust the true riches?"**
> **—Luke 16:11 (KJV)**

The anointing to sponsor the harvest is not random—it rests on those who are faithful, generous, and obedient to divine prompting.

Harvest Sponsors Are Kingdom Catalysts

Without sponsors, many of the greatest revivals and mission movements would have remained visions. When you fund the gospel, you act as a catalyst, accelerating the spread of salvation.

> **"And how shall they preach, except they be sent?"** — **Romans 10:15 (KJV)**

The sender shares in the reward of the sent. Sponsors may never stand on a platform, but they stand behind every soul reached, every church planted, and every life transformed.

The Blessing on Harvest Sponsors Is Supernatural

Those who sponsor the harvest—those who financially support evangelism, missions, church planting, and discipleship—walk under a distinct supernatural blessing. God doesn't overlook those

Money and the Harvest

who fund His work. In fact, He places a multiplied measure of favor on those who invest in what matters most to Him: souls.

God may not call everyone to preach, but He calls many to empower the preaching. If you've said yes to sponsoring the gospel, you haven't just become a giver—you've become a partner in heaven's agenda. And heaven rewards its partners well.

1. God Protects Those Who Fund His Mission

Those who release their resources for the sake of the gospel enter into a divine covenant of protection. Their obedience places a demand on heaven for covering, favor, and supernatural security—because what they are sponsoring is sacred.

Scriptures:

- "Because you have made the Lord… your dwelling place, no evil shall befall you…" —Psalm 91:9–10 (NKJV)

- "The generous will themselves be blessed, for they share their food with the poor." —Proverbs 22:9 (NIV)

- "A generous person will prosper; whoever refreshes others will be refreshed." —Proverbs 11:25 (NIV)

Application: When you prioritize God's mission, He prioritizes your protection.

2. God Multiplies the Resources of Harvest Sponsors

When you give into kingdom work—especially toward reaching the lost—God responds by multiplying your seed. He not only replenishes what you give; He increases it. Why? Because He has found someone who won't hoard the harvest but will release it again.

Scriptures:

- "...he who supplies seed to the sower...will also supply and increase your store of seed and will enlarge the harvest of your righteousness." —2 Corinthians 9:10 (NIV)

- "Give, and it will be given to you... pressed down, shaken together, and running over..." —Luke 6:38 (NIV)

- "The Lord will open the heavens, the storehouse of His bounty... to bless all the work of your hands." —Deuteronomy 28:12 (NIV)

Application: You don't lose when you give—you multiply when you sponsor souls.

3. God Honors Harvest Sponsors Publicly and Privately

God honors those who honor His cause. Those who sow into the harvest may do so quietly, but their reward is both spiritual and visible. Favor will follow you into rooms you didn't expect, and doors will open that you never knocked on.

Scriptures:

- "Those who honor me I will honor, but those who despise me will be disdained." —1 Samuel 2:30b (NIV)

Money and the Harvest

- "Then your Father, who sees what is done in secret, will reward you." —Matthew 6:4 (NIV)

- "A generous person will prosper…" —Proverbs 11:25 (NIV)

Application: Your quiet seed will bring loud blessings.

4. Harvest Sponsors Receive Spiritual Inheritance

You may never step on the mission field, but when you fund the mission, you share in the reward. Souls that are saved, churches that are planted, and lives that are transformed are credited to your account in eternity.

Scriptures:

- "Whoever welcomes a prophet as a prophet will receive a prophet's reward." —Matthew 10:41 (NIV)

- "Not that I desire your gifts; what I desire is that more be credited to your account." —Philippians 4:17 (NIV)

- "The fruit of the righteous is a tree of life, and he who wins souls is wise." —Proverbs 11:30 (NKJV)

Application: Every soul reached through your seed becomes part of your eternal legacy.

5. *God Raises Harvest Sponsors as Kingdom Financiers*

When God finds someone He can trust with kingdom resources, He raises them up as a kingdom financier. These are people with divine strategies, increase, and ideas—not for their own glory, but to resource revivals and fund global missions.

Scriptures:

- "I am the Lord your God, who teaches you to profit, who leads you by the way you should go." —Isaiah 48:17 (NKJV)

- "But remember the Lord your God, for it is He who gives you the ability to produce wealth…" —Deuteronomy 8:18 (NIV)

- "You will be enriched in every way so that you can be generous on every occasion…" —2 Corinthians 9:11 (NIV)

Application: God doesn't bless kingdom sponsors just to increase them—but to expand His reach through them.

God Rewards Those Who Fuel the Gospel

To sponsor the harvest is to step into divine partnership with God's greatest priority—souls. It is more than philanthropy. It is more than giving. It is a spiritual position of influence, favor, and supernatural covering.

You are not just helping—You are building.

You are not just funding—You are planting.

You are not just giving—You are fulfilling the great commission.

And for that, the blessing on your life will be supernatural.

When you give into the harvest, God releases favor, protection, and divine return. The Philippians sowed into Paul's ministry, and he declared a powerful blessing over them:

> **"But my God shall supply all your need according to his riches in glory by Christ Jesus." —Philippians 4:19 (KJV)**

This was not a general promise—it was specifically for those who sponsored the mission. The same blessing is available to faithful sponsors today.

God Honors Sacrificial Sponsorship

True sponsorship isn't always comfortable—it often involves sacrifice. But God sees what is done in secret and rewards openly.

> **"And Jesus sat over against the treasury, and beheld how the people cast money into the treasury... And there came a certain poor widow..." —Mark 12:41–44 (KJV)**

The widow gave out of her lack and caught heaven's attention. Sacrificial sponsorship isn't about the amount—it's about obedience and trust.

Sponsorship is Warfare Against Mammon

When you give strategically, you break the power of mammon. You declare, *"Money is my servant, not my master,"* and your giving becomes a weapon for the kingdom.

> "**Every man according as he purposeth in his heart, so let him give...for God loveth a cheerful giver.**" —2 Corinthians 9:7 (KJV)

Joyful, Spirit-led giving destroys the grip of greed and fear and ushers in revival power.

You May Be the Answer to Someone's Assignment

Many ministries are waiting for breakthrough funding to begin the work God has called them to. Your obedience could be the key.

> "**And the Lord gave the people favour... so that they lent unto them such things as they required. And they spoiled the Egyptians.**" —Exodus 12:36 (KJV)

Before Israel left Egypt, God transferred wealth into their hands for the journey ahead. You may be holding the answer to someone else's mission.

Harvest Sponsors Leave Eternal Legacies

When you give to fund the harvest, you're not just blessing this generation—you're investing in eternity. Your name may never be known on earth, but your reward will echo in heaven.

> "**And they that be wise shall shine as the brightness of the firmament; and they that turn many to righteousness as the stars for ever and ever.**" —Daniel 12:3 (KJV)

Every soul reached through your giving becomes part of your legacy.

Money and the Harvest

Reflection Questions

1. Are you willing to be used by God to fund the harvest?

2. Do you see your resources as tools for eternal impact?

3. Are you praying about where and how God wants you to sponsor His mission?

Prayer

Lord, anoint me to be a harvest sponsor. I surrender all I have to Your purpose. Use my hands to fund the gospel, send missionaries, plant churches, and reach the lost. Let me be trusted with kingdom wealth and guided by Your Spirit. May my giving reflect Your heart and leave an eternal impact. In Jesus' name. Amen.

Chapter 14

The Church That Funds the Harvest

A church is not measured by the size of its building, the beauty of its sanctuary, or the number of its members—it is measured by its commitment to the mission of Christ. A harvest-focused church does more than gather—it gives. It doesn't just host programs—it sends people. When a church becomes a funding center for the great commission, it becomes a powerful extension of heaven on earth.

The Early Church Was a Sending Church

From its inception, the church was a missional movement. The book of Acts reveals that the early church was generous, sacrificial, and committed to funding the spread of the gospel.

> **"And sold their possessions and goods, and parted them to all men, as every man had need...And the Lord added to the church daily such as should be saved." —Acts 2:45, 47 (KJV)**

Their giving wasn't optional—it was integral to revival. They didn't wait for outsiders to support the mission. The church funded it with joy and urgency.

Pastor Dr. Claudine Benjamin

A Harvest Church Builds a Harvest Budget

Too many churches allocate most of their resources to buildings, events, and inward-focused programs. A church that funds the harvest intentionally sets aside money to reach souls.

> "For where your treasure is, there will your heart be also."
> —Matthew 6:21 (KJV)

A harvest budget reflects a harvest burden. Evangelism, missions, outreach, and church planting should be priority line items, not afterthoughts.

The Church Must Lead by Example

If the people are to be givers, the church must model generosity. Leadership must reflect financial integrity and vision that inspires sowing.

> "In all things shewing thyself a pattern of good works…"
> —Titus 2:7 (KJV)

> "Let your light so shine before men, that they may see your good works, and glorify your Father…" —Matthew 5:16 (KJV)

When pastors and leaders give sacrificially, the congregation will follow. Revival generosity begins in the pulpit before it reaches the pews.

A Funding Church Is a Sending Church

The church was never meant to be a monument—it was designed to be a mission base. A church that does not fund the harvest cannot fully fulfill the great commission. Prayer and preaching are essential, but so is provision. The power to send is directly tied to the willingness to give.

In Acts, the church prayed, fasted, laid hands, and sent, but they also gave. A church that funds the work of evangelism, discipleship, and missions becomes a launching pad for souls to be saved, leaders to be raised, and the gospel to be preached across the earth.

1. Sending Requires Supporting

The early church didn't just bless and release—they resourced and released. Paul, Barnabas, Silas, and others were sustained by the generosity of the church. Without financial support, there would have been no missionary journeys, no churches planted, and no letters written.

Scriptures:

- **"…after they had fasted and prayed, they placed their hands on them and sent them off." —Acts 13:3 (NIV)**

- **"for even when I was in Thessalonica, you sent me aid more than once when I was in need." —Philippians 4:16 (NIV)**

- **"And how can anyone preach unless they are sent?— Romans 10:15 (NIV)**

Pastor Dr. Claudine Benjamin

Application: If a church wants to send laborers, it must be ready to supply laborers.

2. A Generous Church Becomes a Global Church

When a church becomes a giving church, it extends its reach beyond its walls. A funding church can touch nations, support missionaries, build schools, plant churches, feed the hungry, and respond to disasters—not by presence but through provision.

Scriptures:

- **"You will be enriched in every way so that you can be generous on every occasion..." —2 Corinthians 9:11 (NIV)**

- **"All the believers were one in heart and mind. No one claimed that any of their possessions was their own... there were no needy persons among them." —Acts 4:32–34 (NIV)**

- **"Go into all the world and preach the gospel to all creation." —Mark 16:15 (NIV)**

Application: A funding church has global influence, even with local attendance.

3. Provision Determines Possibility

Many churches have a vision but lack financial obedience. God often withholds greater assignments because He cannot trust the house to steward His resources. When a church faithfully gives and sows into the harvest, God entrusts more vision—and more provision.

Money and the Harvest

Scriptures:

- "From everyone who has been given much, much will be demanded." —Luke 12:48 (NIV)

- "The plans of the diligent lead to profit as surely as haste leads to poverty." —Proverbs 21:5 (NIV)

- "Bring the whole tithe into the storehouse… and see if I will not throw open the floodgates of heaven…" — Malachi 3:10 (NIV)

Application: God releases more through churches that prove faithful with less.

4. Funding Creates Movement

When a church funds evangelism and missions, it becomes a movement-maker. Finances release missionaries, fuel crusades, print Bibles, purchase outreach tools, and sustain full-time ministers. Generosity puts feet on the gospel and breathes life into vision.

Scriptures:

- "So the word of God spread. The number of disciples in Jerusalem increased rapidly…" —Acts 6:7 (NIV)

- "How beautiful are the feet of those who bring good news!" —Romans 10:15 (NIV)

- "Give, and it will be given to you…" —Luke 6:38 (NIV)

Application: A funding church isn't just a gathering—it becomes a launch pad.

5. God Honors Churches That Prioritize the Harvest

When a church gives sacrificially to reach the lost, heaven takes notice. God honors churches that don't just build buildings but build the kingdom. A harvest-minded church experiences God's supernatural provision, protection, and presence.

Scriptures:

- **"Those who honor me I will honor, but those who despise me will be disdained." —1 Samuel 2:30 (NIV)**

- **"Whoever is kind to the poor lends to the Lord, and he will reward them for what they have done." —Proverbs 19:17 (NIV)**

- **"I will pour out a blessing so great you won't have enough room to take it in!" —Malachi 3:10 (NLT)**

Application: God blesses what aligns with His heart—and nothing touches His heart more than souls.

Build to Send, Not Just to Sit

A funding church becomes a sending church. It doesn't exist to entertain—it exists to equip. It doesn't just count members—it counts missions. When a church chooses to invest in the harvest, God invests in that church.

Your giving writes someone's salvation story.

Your sowing funds a sermon in another nation.

Your obedience sends messengers into the field.

You may never go—but your church will send.

The gospel cannot spread without messengers. And messengers cannot go unless they are sent—and sending requires a financial commitment.

> **"And how shall they preach, except they be sent?" —Romans 10:15 (KJV)**

Whether local or global, churches must adopt the mindset: *We are not just a ministry—we are a mission base. We don't just gather saints—we send laborers.*

Tithes and Offerings Empower the Mission

The tithe supports the local house, while offerings extend the reach of the church into communities and nations. Both are essential for building and advancing the kingdom.

> **"Bring ye all the tithes into the storehouse, that there may be meat in mine house…" —Malachi 3:10 (KJV)**

God designed giving not only to sustain His house but to expand His heart to the lost. A funding church is a resourced church, a ready church, and a responsive church.

God Will Increase What He Can Trust

When a church prioritizes the harvest, God increases its influence and resources. Why? Because God funds what funds His mission.

> "He that is faithful in that which is least is faithful also in much…" —Luke 16:10 (KJV)

If a church is faithful with what it has—even if small—God will enlarge its capacity to reach more, give more, and impact more.

Harvest Churches Experience Supernatural Supply

Churches that give generously never lack. God honors those who prioritize souls. He releases supernatural provisions when we fund the gospel.

> "There is that scattereth, and yet increaseth…" —Proverbs 11:24 (KJV)

> "The liberal soul shall be made fat: and he that watereth shall be watered also himself." —Proverbs 11:25 (KJV)

When churches water others, God waters them in return—with growth, favor, resources, and revival.

Harvest-Focused Churches Build Eternal Legacies

Buildings may fade, but the impact of a church that gives to the gospel lasts forever. Every soul saved, every missionary sent, every church planted—these are eternal fruits.

Money and the Harvest

"And he that reapeth receiveth wages, and gathereth fruit unto life eternal…" —John 4:36 (KJV)

A church that funds the harvest writes its legacy in heaven, not just on earth.

Reflection Questions

1. Does your church prioritize the great commission in its budget?

2. Are they more inward-focused or harvest-driven?

3. What can you do to help your church become a funding center for souls?

Prayer

Father, bless our church to be a funding center for Your harvest. Let our giving reflect Your heart. May we never settle for comfort while the world waits for the gospel. Give our leaders vision, wisdom, and courage to prioritize souls. Let our house be a house that sends, supports, and sows for Your glory. In Jesus' name. Amen.

Chapter 15

The Eternal Return on Investment

In the natural world, people invest in stocks, property, or businesses expecting a return. But the greatest return on investment is not measured in dollars—it is measured in souls, obedience, and eternal reward. When you give to the advancement of the gospel, you are investing in something that will never perish. There is no greater return on investment (ROI) than seeing lives transformed by the power of Jesus Christ.

Kingdom Investments Yield Eternal Dividends

Everything you give to the Lord with the right heart is recorded, remembered, and rewarded by God. Your investment in the gospel produces not just earthly fruit—but heavenly treasure.

> **"But lay up for yourselves treasures in heaven, where neither moth nor rust doth corrupt…"** —Matthew 6:20 (KJV)

> **"For God is not unrighteous to forget your work and labour of love…"** —Hebrews 6:10 (KJV)

While earthly investments are temporary, giving to the Kingdom produces everlasting results.

Pastor Dr. Claudine Benjamin

You Reap What You Sow—In This Life and the Next

The principle of sowing and reaping doesn't just apply to money—it applies to everything you release into God's hands. When you sow into the gospel, the harvest comes both now and in eternity.

> "...he which soweth bountifully shall reap also bountifully." —2 Corinthians 9:6 (KJV)

> "Give, and it shall be given unto you... pressed down, and shaken together, and running over..." —Luke 6:38 (KJV)

Your obedience in giving will yield a multiplied return, not only in provisions but in people coming to Christ.

Souls Are the Most Valuable Return

What does it profit a man to gain the whole world and lose his soul? Conversely, what does it profit when you give and gain souls for eternity? That's the highest form of return.

> "The fruit of the righteous is a tree of life; and he that winneth souls is wise." —Proverbs 11:30 (KJV)

> "...and they that turn many to righteousness shall shine as the stars for ever and ever." —Daniel 12:3 (KJV)

Every dollar you invest in evangelism, missions, and outreach is a seed for souls—a return that cannot be matched by any earthly system.

Heaven Records Eternal Investments

Even if no one applauds your giving or sees your sacrifice, heaven does. God records every offering, every seed, and every act of obedience.

> **"Thy prayers and thine alms are come up for a memorial before God." —Acts 10:4 (KJV)**

Just like Cornelius, your generosity creates a memorial in heaven—an eternal testimony of your faithfulness.

The Judgment Seat of Christ Will Reveal the Return

Every believer will stand before Christ to give an account—not for salvation, but for how they lived and stewarded what they were given.

> **"For we must all appear before the judgment seat of Christ… that every one may receive the things done in his body…" —2 Corinthians 5:10 (KJV)**

> **"Every man's work shall be made manifest… the fire shall try every man's work of what sort it is." —1 Corinthians 3:13 (KJV)**

Only what was done for Christ will last. Only what was sown for His kingdom will remain.

Pastor Dr. Claudine Benjamin

Eternal ROI Comes with Earthly Joy

When you give with kingdom vision, you don't just receive in the next life—you rejoice in this one. There is joy in knowing your giving has eternal value.

> **"It is more blessed to give than to receive." —Acts 20:35 (KJV)**

> **"Rejoice in the Lord always: and again I say, Rejoice." —Philippians 4:4 (KJV)**

A giving heart is a joyful heart—because it knows it is part of something far greater than itself.

Giving Now Shapes Your Eternal Legacy

Every dollar, every act of generosity, and every seed you sow into the kingdom of God becomes part of your eternal legacy. While the world measures success by what you accumulate, heaven measures legacy by what you release. God records every offering, every sacrifice, and every act of faithful giving—not just in accounting books but in eternity's records.

Giving now—while it may feel costly—builds a legacy that time cannot erase, and death cannot stop. What you do with your resources now determines what you will reap forever.

1. Eternal Rewards Are Tied to Earthly Obedience

Your generosity doesn't just bless others—it builds your eternal portfolio. Scripture makes it clear: you are laying up treasures either

Money and the Harvest

on earth or in heaven. When you give now with kingdom purpose, you are investing in forever.

Scriptures:

- "Store up for yourselves treasures in heaven, where moths and vermin do not destroy…" —Matthew 6:20 (NIV)

- "…each of us will give an account of ourselves to God." —Romans 14:12 (NIV)

- "Not that I desire your gifts; what I desire is that more be credited to your account." —Philippians 4:17 (NIV)

Application: Your eternal legacy begins with earthly obedience. You are not just giving for now—you are giving for eternity.

2. What You Give Now Will Greet You in Heaven

You may not see the full impact of your giving on earth—but heaven sees it. One day, you'll meet the souls reached through your sacrifice. Every missionary you funded, every church you helped build, every evangelistic effort you empowered—it will speak for you in eternity.

Scriptures:

- "Then the King will say… 'I was hungry and you gave Me something to eat… whatever you did for one of the least of these… you did for Me.'" —Matthew 25:34–40

(NIV)

- "Your prayers and gifts to the poor have come up as a memorial offering before God." —Acts 10:4 (NIV)

- "The fruit of the righteous is a tree of life; and he that winneth souls is wise." —Proverbs 11:30 (KJV)

Application: Your giving now becomes your welcome later. Souls will thank you that you chose to give when others withheld.

3. **Legacy Is Measured by What You Gave, Not Just What You Built**

True legacy isn't defined by earthly wealth or fame—it's defined by eternal impact. God doesn't just remember how much you had; He remembers how much you gave for His purpose. What you release becomes part of your divine legacy.

Scriptures:

- "…it is more blessed to give than to receive." —Acts 20:35 (NIV)

- "The generous will themselves be blessed, for they share their food with the poor." —Proverbs 22:9 (NIV)

- "A good person leaves an inheritance for their children's children, but a sinner's wealth is stored up for the righteous." —Proverbs 13:22 (NIV)

Money and the Harvest

Application: You may not be remembered for your salary, but you will be remembered for your sacrifice.

4. Your Giving Shapes Generational Impact

When you model a life of kingdom generosity, you leave behind a pattern for your children and spiritual heirs to follow. You teach others to value eternal things over temporal things, and you plant seeds that multiply for generations.

Scriptures:

- **"The righteous man walks in his integrity; His children are blessed after him." —Proverbs 20:7 (NKJV)**

- **"Their children will be mighty in the land; the generation of the upright will be blessed." —Psalm 112:2 (NIV)**

- **"One generation commends your works to another…" —Psalm 145:4 (NIV)**

Application: Your generosity now will influence those who come after you—long after you're gone.

5. God Keeps Record—Even When Others Don't

Your secret giving, your anonymous donations, your quiet obedience—none of it goes unnoticed by heaven. While people may forget, God writes it into your eternal story. Nothing given in faith is ever wasted. Nothing sown in love is ever lost.

Pastor Dr. Claudine Benjamin

Scriptures:

- "...your Father, who sees what is done in secret, will reward you." —Matthew 6:4 (NIV)

- "God is not unjust; he will not forget your work and the love you have shown Him..." —Hebrews 6:10 (NIV)

- "each one's work will become manifest... and fire will test what sort of work each one has done." —1 Corinthians 3:13 (ESV)

Application: You may not see full reward here—but God never forgets faithful sowers.

Legacy is Built One Seed at a Time

Every time you give, you shape eternity. Every offering, every tithe, every act of generosity carves your name into heaven's ledger. When you give now with eternity in mind, you ensure that your life will outlive you—not through buildings or accolades, but through lives changed, souls saved, and a kingdom advanced.

Don't wait for later—give now.
Don't invest only in time—invest in eternity.
Let your legacy be written in souls.
Let your generosity echo forever.

Many people plan for retirement but neglect to plan for eternity. The wise steward is not only preparing for this life but is storing treasure in heaven.

Money and the Harvest

"Well done, thou good and faithful servant… enter thou into the joy of thy lord." —Matthew 25:21 (KJV)

Let it be said of us that we didn't just live well—we gave well, sowed well, and left behind an eternal impact.

Reflection Questions

1. Are you investing more in temporary things or eternal things?

2. Do you view giving as a spiritual investment with kingdom returns?

3. What part of your financial life will still matter 100 years from now?

Prayer

Lord, help me to give with eternity in mind. Let me invest in what will never fade—souls, Your Word, and the mission of the gospel. Teach me to sow in faith, knowing that every gift is recorded in heaven and will bring a return for Your glory. Use me to shape eternity through what I give today. In Jesus' name. Amen.

Conclusion

Giving That Outlives You

There comes a point in every believer's journey when they must decide: *Will I live for today, or will I sow for eternity? Will I build a legacy of temporary comforts, or will I invest in souls, missions, and the move of God that will echo throughout eternity?*

The message of this book is clear: *Money matters to the mission.* Finances are not separate from faith—they are a mirror of our priorities. When surrendered, they become a powerful tool in God's hands to reach the lost, heal the broken, and restore nations.

You Were Born to Fund the Mission

God didn't just save you to survive—He saved you to participate in His redemptive plan for the world. Whether you're a business owner, a pastor, a stay-at-home parent, or a young believer with limited means, you are part of God's economy. What you give matters. What you release multiplies.

> **"Now he that ministereth seed to the sower... multiply your seed sown, and increase the fruits of your righteousness."**
> **—2 Corinthians 9:10 (KJV)**

Pastor Dr. Claudine Benjamin

You were born to sow what God entrusts to you, and through that obedience, help reap the greatest harvest the world has ever seen.

This Is Not Just About Money—It's About Surrender

True giving is not about the amount—it's about the heart. God doesn't measure generosity by numbers but by surrender and sacrifice.

> **"And he looked up, and saw the rich men casting their gifts into the treasury… But she of her penury hath cast in all the living that she had." —Luke 21:1–4 (KJV)**

The widow gave more than the wealthy because she gave with all her heart. You may not feel like you have much—but when you give with faith and joy, God uses it for more than you could ever imagine.

Don't Let Your Giving Die With You—Let It Outlive You

What will remain when you are gone? Will your generosity go with you to the grave, or will it continue speaking on earth and in heaven? A life of impact is not measured by what we consume but by what we release into the hands of God. Every believer has a divine opportunity: to sow in such a way that their giving outlives them and leaves an eternal imprint on the world.

God is looking for legacy-minded givers—those who invest in kingdom work with vision, not just emotion. When your giving is intentional, generational, and mission-driven, it creates a spiritual inheritance that time cannot erase.

1. Godly Giving Doesn't End at the Grave

If your giving stops the moment your life ends, you've missed an opportunity to shape the future. Biblical stewardship includes thinking beyond your lifetime—planning and planting now so that souls, ministries, and missions can be blessed after you're gone.

Scriptures:

- **"A good man leaves an inheritance to his children's children…" —Proverbs 13:22 (NKJV)**

- **"By faith Abel still speaks, even though he is dead." — Hebrews 11:4 (NIV)**

- **"The memory of the righteous is a blessing…" — Proverbs 10:7 (ESV)**

Application: Your giving should not have an expiration date—build systems, support ministries, and leave behind financial seeds that keep bearing fruit.

2. Eternal Impact Requires Intentional Stewardship

Impactful giving doesn't happen by accident—it requires deliberate planning. Whether through planned legacy giving, endowments, estate stewardship, or dedicated seed funds, wise believers ask God not only what to give but how to make it last.

Scriptures:

- "Suppose one of you wants to build a tower. Won't you first sit down and estimate the cost...?" —Luke 14:28 (NIV)

- "The wise store up choice food and olive oil, but fools gulp theirs down." —Proverbs 21:20 (NIV)

- "The plans of the diligent lead surely to abundance..." —Proverbs 21:5 (ESV)

Application: Don't just give emotionally—give strategically. Let your generosity reflect wisdom and foresight.

3. Your Giving Can Sustain Ministries After You're Gone

The churches, missionaries, and ministries you support now can continue winning souls and transforming lives long after you've transitioned—if you've sown wisely. End-time harvest funding doesn't stop with your lifespan. It continues through the foundations you lay today.

Scriptures:

- "Yes," says the Spirit, "they will rest from their labor, for their deeds will follow them." —Revelation 14:13 (NIV)

- "Whoever is kind to the poor lends to the Lord, and he will reward them for what they have done." —Proverbs 19:17 (NIV)

- "The blameless spend their days under the Lord's care, and their inheritance will endure forever." —Psalm 37:18 (NIV)

Application: Set up ways for your giving to keep giving. Fund what God loves—souls, not monuments.

4. Legacy Giving Inspires the Next Generation

When you choose to give with a legacy mindset, you model something powerful to your children, church, and community. You show them what it means to live for eternal things, and you pass on the baton of faith-driven generosity.

Scriptures:

- "One generation shall praise Your works to another, and shall declare Your mighty acts." —Psalm 145:4 (NKJV)

- "Direct your children onto the right path, and when they are older, they will not leave it." —Proverbs 22:6 (NLT)

- "The righteous lead blameless lives; blessed are their children after them." —Proverbs 20:7 (NIV)

Application: Don't just leave behind finances—leave behind a financial legacy rooted in purpose.

5. You Are Called to Give Like an Eternal Investor

Eternal investors think differently. They don't sow for applause—they sow for eternal applause. They don't give for recognition—they give for redemption. Giving with heaven in mind positions you to leave behind a supernatural return that continues long after you've taken your last breath.

Scriptures:

- **"…store up for yourselves treasures in heaven…" — Matthew 6:20 (NIV)**

- **"each one's work will become manifest… the fire will test what sort of work each one has done." —1 Corinthians 3:13 (ESV)**

- **"Well done, good and faithful servant! You have been faithful with a few things…" —Matthew 25:21 (NIV)**

Application: Don't aim for temporary recognition—sow for eternal significance.

Let Your Seed Keep Speaking

What if your giving could outlive your obituary? What if your name faded, but your seed kept multiplying? That's the power of legacy giving. That's the call of a kingdom-minded believer. Your life may have an end date, but your giving doesn't have to. Let it echo through generations. Let it speak when you can't. Let it outlive you.

Don't just give for today—Sow for tomorrow.

Don't let your generosity die with you—Let it ignite revival after you.

The only wealth that outlives you is the wealth you give away. Houses fade, businesses dissolve, and possessions lose value—but every act of obedience, every gospel investment, every seed for souls is written into eternity.

> **"Lay not up for yourselves treasures upon earth… But lay up for yourselves treasures in heaven…" —Matthew 6:19-20 (KJV)**

Let your giving be a declaration: *"I was here—and I made a difference for the kingdom of God."*

Your Obedience Will Reach People You'll Never Meet

The seed you plant may reach a soul in Africa, fund a revival in your city, or sponsor a missionary who will preach to thousands. You may never see their faces on earth—but they will greet you in eternity.

> **"And he that reapeth receiveth wages, and gathereth fruit unto life eternal…" —John 4:36 (KJV)**

One act of giving can change a generation. One offering can shift a nation. One obedient heart can release revival.

This Is Your Moment

Now is the time to shift your focus from financial survival to kingdom impact. Now is the time to ask, *"Lord, how can I give to what You love most—souls?"* Now is the time to partner with heaven's agenda and become a steward God can trust.

Final Commissioning Declaration

*"Lord, I am Yours. All I have belongs to You.
I surrender my money, mindset, and means.
Make me a faithful steward and a joyful giver.
Let my resources reach the nations.
Let my obedience fund the gospel.
Let my generosity outlive me.
I commit to sowing into the harvest—until every soul is reached, every ear hears, and every nation knows.
In Jesus' name. Amen."*

Harvest Declarations and Promises

Daily Declarations of Faith and Provision

I declare that I am a faithful steward of all that God has entrusted to me.

> "Moreover it is required in stewards, that a man be found faithful." —1 Corinthians 4:2 (KJV)

I declare that I will sow generously and reap bountifully.

> "...he which soweth bountifully shall reap also bountifully." —2 Corinthians 9:6 (KJV)

I declare that my seed is making an eternal impact and bringing in the harvest.

> "...he that reapeth receiveth wages, and gathereth fruit unto life eternal." —John 4:36 (KJV)

I declare that I am a kingdom financer—called to fund the gospel and bless the nations.

> "But thou shalt remember the Lord thy God: for it is he that giveth thee power to get wealth." —Deuteronomy 8:18 (KJV)

I declare that every seed I sow is multiplied and returned with overflow.

> "Give, and it shall be given unto you…running over…" — Luke 6:38 (KJV)

I declare that I will not serve mammon—I serve God alone.

> "Ye cannot serve God and mammon." —Matthew 6:24 (KJV)

I declare that my church will be a sending and funding church for the end-time harvest.

> "Go ye therefore, and teach all nations…" —Matthew 28:19 (KJV)

I declare that I give with joy, without fear or withholding.

> "God loveth a cheerful giver." —2 Corinthians 9:7 (KJV)

I declare that I live under an open heaven, and God supplies all my needs.

> "Bring ye all the tithes… I will… open you the windows of heaven…" —Malachi 3:10 (KJV)

I declare that my giving builds a legacy that outlives me.

> "A good man leaveth an inheritance to his children's children…" —Proverbs 13:22 (KJV)

Harvest Promises from God's Word

Provision Promise:

> "But my God shall supply all your need according to his riches in glory by Christ Jesus." Philippians 4:19 (KJV)

Increase Promise:

> "There is that scattereth, and yet increaseth…" —Proverbs 11:24 (KJV)

Eternal Reward Promise:

> "…they that turn many to righteousness shall shine as the stars for ever…" —Daniel 12:3 (KJV)

Seed Promise:

> "Now he that ministereth seed to the sower… multiply your seed sown…" —2 Corinthians 9:10 (KJV)

Abundance Promise:

> "Thou shalt surely give… and the Lord thy God shall bless thee in all thy works…" —Deuteronomy 15:10 (KJV)

Harvest Promise:

> "Lift up your eyes… for they are white already to harvest." —John 4:35 (KJV)

Legacy Promise:

"The fruit of the righteous is a tree of life." —Proverbs 11:30 (KJV)

Call to Action: Your Hands Hold the Answer

You may never stand on a foreign field
You may never preach to thousands
You may never plant a church or write a sermon
But when you give—you are part of the mission.

Your giving sends the messenger
Your obedience opens the door
Your sacrifice reaches the soul
Heaven moves when you release what's in your hand.

Let this journey stir your faith, ignite your generosity, and position your finances to fulfill the purpose of God.

You are not just a giver—you are a kingdom investor.
You are not just supporting the work—you are shaping eternity.
Now, let us rise and finance the mission of God.

Scripture and Reference Index

God's Ownership and Provision

- Psalm 24:1
- Haggai 2:8
- Deuteronomy 8:18
- Philippians 4:19

Stewardship and Faithfulness

- 1 Corinthians 4:2
- Luke 16:10–11
- Proverbs 3:5–6

Sowing, Reaping, and Generosity

- 2 Corinthians 9:6
- Galatians 6:7
- Proverbs 11:24–25
- Luke 6:38

Tithes, Offerings, and Kingdom Giving

- Malachi 3:10
- 1 Corinthians 9:14
- Matthew 6:21

The Great Commission and Gospel Funding

- Matthew 28:19–20
- Romans 10:14–15
- Acts 1:8

Breaking Financial Bondage

- Proverbs 22:7
- Romans 13:8
- Ecclesiastes 11:4

Mammon vs. God's Spirit

- Matthew 6:24
- 1 Timothy 6:10
- Luke 12:15

Revival and Generous Living

- Acts 2:44–47
- Acts 4:32–35
- Proverbs 3:9

Eternal Rewards and Kingdom Investment

- Matthew 6:19–20
- Daniel 12:3
- 1 Corinthians 3:13

Legacy, Sacrifice, and Obedience

- Luke 21:1–4
- Acts 10:4
- Matthew 25:21

www.ingramcontent.com/pod-product-compliance
Lightning Source LLC
Chambersburg PA
CBHW050820160426
43192CB00010B/1831